KINSMAN AVENUE PUBLISHING, INC.
www.kinsmanquarterly.org

Registered with the U.S. Library of Congress

Printed in the United States of America

Library of Congress Control Number: Pending

Holiday Plays for Cultures Worldwide

Cover Design: Monique Franz

Interior Design: Danah Lassiter and Monique Franz

Edited by Danah Lassiter

Contributing Playwrights: Russell Nichols, Rohan Magerman, Maya De La Torre, Louis DeVaughn Nelson, Matthew J. Kaplan, Yangzhou (Yao) Bian, Melanie Payne, Maximillian Gill, James McLindon, Mark Sbani, Achiro P. Olwoch, Sofía Méndez Ramírez, Samara Siskind, Jeremy Rafal, Paul Bowman, and Emma Denson

HOLIDAY PLAYS
for Cultures Worldwide

Edited by Danah Lassiter

17 SHORT SCRIPTS FOR SMALL CASTS

Playwrights: Achiro P. Olwoch, Emma Denson, James McLindon,
Jeremy Rafal, Louis DeVaughn Nelson, Mark Sbani, Matthew J. Kaplan,
Maya De La Torre, Maximillian Gill, Melanie Payne, Paul Bowman,
Rohan Magerman, Russell Nichols, Samara Siskind,
Sofía Méndez Ramírez, and Yangzhou (Yao) Bian.

EDITOR'S NOTE

Theatre has always held a mirror to the world — sometimes reflecting it with startling clarity, other times distorting it just enough to reveal truths we might otherwise overlook. The plays in this collection do both. They speak to the moment we're in, yet echo across time and place. They remind us why the stage remains one of the most potent spaces for human imagination and conviction.

This collection is not just a gathering of scripts — it's an archive of voices in motion. Each play offers a world of its own: characters who love, rage, question, fall apart, or hope for something new. Whether intimate or epic, grounded or surreal, these works ask urgent questions about who we are, what we value, and ultimately how we live.

Some plays will sit quietly with you; others will jolt you out of your seat. All of them are meant to be read aloud, embodied, wrestled with. For actors and directors, this is fertile ground. For readers and thinkers, it's a feast of language, structure, and emotional truth. At a time when attention is fleeting and understanding is scarce, these plays sound an alarm. They ask us to stop, to listen, and to feel it all. These plays remind us that, even in darkness, the stage offers light.

Welcome to the conversation.

Danah Lassiter

For those who have earth-shattering things to say.

A special thank you to the Kinsman Avenue Publishing team and all the featured playwrights for trusting me with their work.

Many thanks.

TABLE OF CONTENTS

Holiday	*Title* and Playwright	Page

AMERICA! THE GAME

A Play in One Act

by

Russell Nichols

Cast of Characters

Baller: The basketball phenom.

Trader: The Wall Street suit.

Rapper: The antisocial emcee.

Player: The smooth operator.

Hustler: The low-level dealer.

SCENE
Game Board

TIME
Game Time

SETTING: The Rule Book a.k.a. Production Notes:
                                  Urban legend says that every July 4th, a
                                  secret society gathers in an undisclosed
                                  location to play a game. Welcome to America!
                                  The Game — an absurd, surreal live-action
                                  board game experience. The stage: Minimal
                                  with oversized game elements to emphasize
                                  the sense of entrapment. The pieces: Each
                                  actor wears a distinct red and/or white
                                  and/or blue costume with a relevant prop.
                                  The effects: Prioritize sound to create
                                  atmosphere. Movements on the board are
                                  mechanical. The world is both playful and
                                  oppressive, caught between a "fun-for-
                                  the-whole-family" game and an inescapable
                                  reality.

AT RISE: In the darkness, the sound of dice
                                  tumbling on a board echoes like rolling
                                  thunder. Then unseen movement. Shuffling.
                                  Followed by voices.

                         TRADER
Unhand me!

                         BALLER
Fool, I ain't touch you.

                         TRADER
I'm not talking to you, am I?

                         PLAYER
Y'all mind turning down the volume? A brother's tryna get his
beauty rest on.

                         TRADER
How can you sleep at a time like this?

                         PLAYER
Watch me.

                    (Lights up. Four men stand at various
                    spots   on   stage   in   a   staggered
                    arrangement from stage right to left.)

                    (RAPPER, in a tracksuit, holds a
                    pen and jots lyrics on his hand,
                    mumbling to himself. TRADER rocks a
                    power suit, the financial pages under
                    his arm. BALLER wears a jersey and
                    shorts, and spins a basketball on
                    his finger. PLAYER, in a tank top and
                    durag, tries to sleep standing up.
                    It might not be clear just yet, but
                    these men are human-sized pieces on a
                    giant game board.)

                         TRADER
I can't hear myself think with all that rappity-rap.
                    (to rapper)
Hey, Jay-Z — yoo-hoo! You wanna knock it off?

                         RAPPER
                    (rapping)
Knock, knock, who's there but the devil in a suit. Tryna profit off
the world while embezzling the truth.

                         BALLER
Leave Rapper alone. He ain't hurting nobody.

                         TRADER
Oh, my ears bleed to differ!

                         PLAYER
Take it easy, baby. My man's over here letting his creative juices
flow freely. What are you doing, Trader?

                         TRADER
I am trying to figure out how to get out of this hellhole,
thankyouverymuch.

                         BALLER
How about you get that stick out your butthole, thankyouverymuch.

                         TRADER
                    (flaps open the paper)
Pfft! I have no time for such buffoonery.

                    (A moment of quiet, then the dice
                    roll. TRADER groans.)

                         BALLER
               (looking up)
Here we go again.

               (All eyes turn to PLAYER as an invisible
               hand pushes him one space forward,
               then two spaces back. PLAYER resists
               to no avail.)

                         PLAYER
               (to the heavens)
Yo, slow your roll! A brother just got comfortable!

                         TRADER
And that is exactly where you went wrong, Player.

                         BALLER
Say, Mr. Wall Street, I suggest you void that check-writing mouth
of yours before I—

                         TRADER
What? You "deposit" your foot in my derriere?
               (BALLER lunges at TRADER to no avail.)
Transaction declined!

                         RAPPER
               (rapping)
No balance in my account, I'm surrounded by green houses. But I'm
rapping gold bars, put the money where my mouth is.

                         BALLER
Shhh! Ya'll heard that?

               (The pieces listen.)

                         PLAYER
               (fixing himself up)
Ooh ooh, sounds like we got some new, new coming in.

               (The noise repeats: unseen movement.
               Shuffling. Followed by another voice.)

                         HUSTLER (O.S.)
Get your hands off me!

(The pieces look around, trying to keep cool as an invisible hand slides a new piece onto the board: HUSTLER, in a hoodie and joggers. HUSTLER resists. He gets pushed to the first space, stage right. And he's freaking all the way out.)

                    BALLER
A new piece? That's what I'm talking 'bout!

                    HUSTLER
Wh-wh-where am I? What is this?!

                    TRADER
          (back to reading)
The end of the world.

                    HUSTLER
What?!

                    PLAYER
Baby, don't pay no mind to tighty whities. What's your name?

                    HUSTLER
Me? I'm...I...

                    BALLER
Check the tag. In your hoodie.
          (BALLER motions to his tag.)
Should have your name on it.

                    HUSTLER
          (checking tag)
"Made In America."

                    PLAYER
The other side.

                    HUSTLER
Hustler?

                    PLAYER
Okay, I see you, Hustler. It's been a minute since we've had the pleasure of a new piece.

                         HUSTLER
A piece? What is this? Who are you?

                         PLAYER
Well, if you couldn't tell from all this charm oozing out of a
brother's pores, I'm Player.

                         BALLER
And I'm Baller.

                         RAPPER
                    (rapping)
And I'm sick and tired of being sick and tired. It was written,
still I'm getting by, spitting fire.

                         BALLER
That's Rapper. And that gentleman with the gigantic pole protruding
from his rectal orifice is Trader.

                    (TRADER turns a page of his paper,
                    dismissively.)

                         HUSTLER
                    (nauseated)
I don't understand what...
                    (The   dice   rolls.   The   invisible
                    hand   moves   HUSTLER   three   spaces
                    forward,   then   two   back   against   his
                    discombobulated will.)
What is...I can't...
                    (dawning)
Am I in hell?

          PLAYER   TRADER
     I'm too sexy for hell.   Indubitably.

          BALLER   RAPPER
     That's up in the air.   (rapping)
                                         It's a cold world, feel
                                         the heat from the flames.
                                         No resting in peace when
                                         you a piece in the game.

                         HUSTLER
I'm not supposed to be here!

                              TRADER
And yet, here you are...Hustler, was it?

                              HUSTLER
No, no, no, I'm not a hustler, I'm a...I'm a...

                              BALLER
Lemme guess: You were grubbing at a Fourth of July cookout when you
got snatched up, right?

                              HUSTLER
What? No, I was in my kitchen, filling baggies with sour candies,
about to take my son to see the fireworks—

                              PLAYER
Sweet. Then you heard a loud voice from the heavens.

                              HUSTLER
Yeah, it came outta nowhere! Like thunder. And it asked me if I
wanted to "play America!"

                              BALLER
And what'd you say?

                              HUSTLER
What'd I say?!

                              PLAYER
Did you give your consent to the role play?

                              BALLER
Did you say yes?

                              HUSTLER
No! I didn't say anything. I didn't know what I was hearing!
                    (clutching his head)
I—I couldn't even think.

                              TRADER
You'll fit right in.

                              HUSTLER
Next thing I know I'm here...wherever here is.

PLAYER

Trust, baby, we know the feeling. That tingling sensation that takes over your whole body like <u>oowee</u>.

BALLER

You're disoriented, but it'll pass, Hustler.

HUSTLER

I told you, I'm not a hustler! I'm a—

BALLER

Bruh, whoever you used to be, that's last season stuff.

PLAYER

Your identity's a little wobbly to start, but just be cool. Once the memory fades, you'll slide in nice and easy.

BALLER

Like me, for instance—

HUSTLER

Like you?

BALLER
(does fancy dribbling)
Couldn't tell you who I was before, but now? I'm an all-American, up-and-coming superstar. Filthy handle with a forty-inch vert. Jumper so wet, you'd need galoshes.

RAPPER
(rapping)
The past is washed away in high tides of lost history. We play to survive, how to thrive remains a mystery.

PLAYER
(whipping out a container of arousal
gel and doing a sensual dance)
And yours truly? I'm a paragon of pasión, fluent in body language, who knows how to please and please—

TRADER

Oh, please!

PLAYER

Alas, we have a Player hater among us.

                         HUSTLER
                    (to TRADER)
And who are you? A lawyer?

                         TRADER
I'm rich, is what I am. A day trader with an eye to discern the
difference between a winner...
                    (pointed)
...and a whiner.

                         BALLER
Just pretend he ain't even here.

                         HUSTLER
                    (whining)
I don't wanna be here.

                         BALLER
Baby, that ship has sailed. So what's your hustle, Hustler?

                         HUSTLER
Stop calling me that!

                         BALLER
What you pushing? Rocks? Pills? Powder?

                         HUSTLER
I push nothing! I—I've never sold drugs in my life!
                    (BALLER motions to HUSTLER's hoodie.
                    HUSTLER fishes in his pocket. Panicking.
                    His eyes bulge. He pulls out a bag of
                    white powder.)
Nah, nah, this ain't mine!

                         BALLER
                    (spins basketball)
You come with a prop. It's all in the game.

                         PLAYER
                    (re: his prop)
I got the lube...Trust, we know the situation looks real sticky,
but the best you can do is keep your head up, your voice down and
try to survive long as you can.

                         HUSTLER
                    (horrified looks to heaven)
Help!

TRADER

For crying out loud.

HUSTLER

Look, I can't be here! I got a son. I'm supposed be taking him to see the fireworks—

TRADER

Oh, really? This son of yours, what's his name?

HUSTLER

My son? His name is...No, I know his name, of course I know his name. It's, uh...
                    (smacking his head)
Ahhh!

BALLER

Don't beat yourself up, bruh.
                    (The dice rolls. BALLER moves four
                    spaces forward, then five back. He
                    doesn't fight it.)
We've all been played.

RAPPER

                    (rapping)
Makes you wonder how we keep from going under. Stakes high, cheat dice rolling like thunder.

TRADER

Speak for yourself. I didn't get played. I'm playing to win.

BALLER

Win what, negro?

TRADER

I am a top-tier capitalist.

BALLER

With a capital cap.

TRADER

This game might be a sunk cost for the likes of you peasants, but me? Pfft. This is child's play to me.

BALLER

You so smart, how come you ain't broke out then?

                              TRADER
Because—you sweaty sideshow act—beating the market is a matter of
timing.

                              PLAYER
Well it's high time you slippity-slide off that high horse.

                              TRADER
I will do no such thing.

                              HUSTLER
But none of this is real! That's what y'all keep telling me. We're
all getting played, right? So that suit, those shoes, your "success"
— it's all fake. It's a role you bought into.
              (TRADER opens the paper, ignoring
              HUSTLER's tirade.)
And that paper's blank!

              (TRADER reads regardless.)

                              BALLER
You better listen to the rookie. It don't matter who you think you
are, or how much you think you made. At the end of the day, you a
piece on this board. Just like us.

                              TRADER
Ha! I'm nothing like you, losers.

                              PLAYER
Not even these devastating good looks of mine can dodge the fact
that we're all headed to the same place.

                              HUSTLER
Wait, whatchu mean by that?
              (The pieces point offstage. HUSTLER
              stares offstage.)
What happens?
              (silence)
What happens at the end?!
              (silence)
We can't just stand here and wait around! We-we gotta do something,
we gotta act!

              (The dice rolls. RAPPER moves forward
              two spaces, then three back.)

                              RAPPER
                    (rapping)
I lie awake, anticipate if the die should seal my fate. On this
board, no escape, I pray the Lord my soul to take.

                              HUSTLER
No, no, no, no, I'm not doing this. I'm not part of this, I'm
leaving, I'm out!

                              PLAYER
Ooh, I like the fire, but walking away ain't an option.

                              HUSTLER
                    (foot down)
I will not be moved!

                    (The dice rolls. The invisible hand
                    slides HUSTLER forward a space, then
                    back two. HUSTLER resists to no
                    avail.)

                              RAPPER
The cost of living in this "indivisible land" is at the mercy of
the damn invisible hand.

                              HUSTLER
                    (forlorn)
What if I pray real hard?

                              PLAYER
Ha, that's old school.

                              BALLER
Throwback.

                              TRADER
Bear trap.

                              BALLER
Another piece tried that move. Before you came. Preacher.

                              PLAYER
Oowee, my man's was praying his holy heart out.

                              HUSTLER
What happened to him?
                    (The pieces point offstage. HUSTLER
                    looks horrified.)
What if I make a run for it?

                              BALLER
Give it your best shot.
                    (HUSTLER looks around. Crouches down.
                    Ready, set, go! He bolts, but the
                    invisible hand snatches him back to
                    his spot.)
We tried everything, bruh. No dice.

                              HUSTLER
                    (HUSTLER slumps down, defeated.
                    Speaks to himself.)
No dice...no dice...That's it!

                              TRADER
Oh, how I loathe the smell of a harebrained scheme.

                              HUSTLER
The dice! The dice controls our movements! So check this out. What
if we make our own dice?

                              TRADER
And how, pray tell, do you plan to do that? Turn your fairy dust
into magic blocks?

                              HUSTLER
I, uh...you're right. I got nothing.

                              BALLER
See? The problem is, we be spending so much time going at each
other. Where the teamwork at, huh?
                    (muted response)
Now, me personally? I think Hustler's onto something.

                              TRADER
Color me surprised.

                              PLAYER
I mean, I know a lil' sumthin sumthin about custom dice when it
comes to lovemaking, but not game-breaking.

                    BALLER
            (looks at basketball)
I mean, we can't move, but maybe...
            (looks at the other pieces)
Trader, toss your paper to Rapper.

                    TRADER
And why should I?

                    PLAYER
It's all love, man. Just slide that thing over.

            (TRADER huffs, but complies, tossing
            the paper to RAPPER.)

                    BALLER
Rapper, you got the prop pen, so you can write—

                    PLAYER
You wanna enlighten a brother to the play right quick?

                    BALLER
Look, we can't move on our own. But what if, like Hustler said, we
make our own dice? We can use our props to—

                    HUSTLER
—to send a message!

                    BALLER
Bingo.

                    PLAYER
Ooh, that's smooth.

                    TRADER
Actually not too shabby.

                    BALLER
So Rapper writes, and I'll...Player, throw me that lube.

                    PLAYER
Whoa, whoa, what part of the game is that?!

                    BALLER
I need something sticky. For the message.

                    PLAYER
This is water-based.

                    BALLER
And unlike me, it's way past its prime. So at this point, I'm
guessing that stuff is super-duper glue.
                    (Disgusted, PLAYER chucks the lube.
                    BALLER catches it. Smears the sticky
                    residue over the ball.)
You almost done, Rapper?

                    RAPPER
                    (RAPPER stares at the blank page.
                    He's blocked.)
I can't write.

                    HUSTLER
Just ask for help.

                    RAPPER
I...don't know how.

                    TRADER
                    (throwing up his hands)
Another bust.

                    HUSTLER
I don't hear you coming up with anything.

                    TRADER
I do not write rhymes. I write forecasts.

                    BALLER
Well, you always talking 'bout how you "beat the market." How 'bout
you drop a stock beat for us?

                         (TRADER scoffs. But the pieces stare
                         at him. Under pressure, TRADER
                         beatboxes. And the beat is fire! The
                         other pieces bounce, hyping up blocked
                         RAPPER.)

                    RAPPER
                    (rapping)
If there's anybody out there, we could use support. This dangerous
game is a full-contact sport.

                         BALLER
That's what I'm talkin—

                         RAPPER
                    (rapping)
Five brothers on a board in desperate need of help. Losing our
minds ain't the best for mental health.

                         PLAYER
Bars! See, I knew you—

                         RAPPER
                    (rapping)
Every one step forward be like two steps back. Go figure, the
spinner's rigged like a set trap.

                         HUSTLER
That's dope, now let's write—

                         RAPPER
                    (rapping)
Born in a space in a race we didn't choose. America! The Game was
made for us to lose.

                    (The pieces go wild. RAPPER nods,
                    feeling himself as he scribbles the
                    lyrics. Folds up the paper, tosses it
                    to BALLER. BALLER presses the message
                    to the sticky basketball.)

                         BALLER
Alright then, we're good to go, my guys—

                         HUSTLER
Wait, what about this powder?

         PLAYER   TRADER
    Uh-uh, keep that to   I don't dabble in
    yourself, playboy.   depreciating assets.

         BALLER   RAPPER
    Yo, I got endorsements.   Don't hand me no nose
                                 candy.

                         HUSTLER
              (emptying the baggie and speaking to
              himself)
Candy...sour candies...fireworks...
              (then: an epiphany)
Tabari!
              (choking up)
That's my-that's my son's name. His name is Tabari—
              (hollers)
TABARI!

              (The pieces nod at him,
              respectfully.)

                         TRADER
              (back to business)
Yeah, so um, now what, Big Baller?

                         BALLER
              (looking at audience)
You said it yourself, Trader: It's all a matter of timing. So all
we can do is roll...

              (BALLER rolls the ball offstage. The
              pieces stand there, watching as it
              goes off into the unknown.)

                    (BLACKOUT)

                    (END OF PLAY)

BENEATH THE MINSTRELS' FOOTSTEPS

A Play in One Act

by

Rohan Magerman

Cast of Characters

<u>Trudy</u>:	Female, late 50s, Coloured[1], a proud, no-nonsense, but caring woman who leads the Jolly Jives troupe.
<u>Cardo</u>:	Male, 13, Coloured, Trudy's son, making his debut in the Cape Town Minstrel Carnival[2].
<u>Mr. White</u>:	Male, 30s, Caucasian, manager of The Meridian Hotel, with concerns about the parade's noise.
<u>Abe Solomons</u>:	Male, 40s, Coloured, a member of the Carnival's board, trying to mediate between the two sides.
<u>Young Trudy</u>:	Female, 13-15, Coloured, dressed in a Kaapse Klopse outfit, with a spirited, joyful energy.
<u>Young Abe</u>:	Male, 13-15, Coloured, dressed in a Kaapse Klopse outfit, with a spirited, joyful energy.

<u>SCENE</u>
Cape Town, South Africa

<u>TIME</u>
Early January and Second New Year

[1] A South African ethnic group.
[2] Tweede Nuwe Jaar (Second New Year): A colourful parade held annually in Cape Town on January 2nd.

SETTING: Cape Town, South Africa.

AT RISE: TRUDY occupies a lone couch, hunched over her needlework. Her hands move with quiet concentration as she sews a colourful, glittering blazer draped over her lap. There is a Christmas tree behind her. From offstage left, we hear CARDO practicing, Daar Kom Die Alibama[3] on a trombone. TRUDY holds up the blazer, turns it in her hands, examines the seams like it holds something more than just fabric. Then - bang! A thunderous noise explodes from offstage right. Her head jerks up.

TRUDY

Those kids again!
> (TRUDY rises from the couch, moves toward the edge of the stage, and shouts a warning to the unseen kids outside, offstage right.)

You kids stop kicking that ball around here before you break my window! I see one crack and I'm telling' your parents, you hear me? Go find a field or something!
> (Returning to the couch, she picks up the blazer and calls out to offstage left.)

Cardo! Ri-car-do!

> (The trombone cuts off mid-note. After a pause, CARDO responds from offstage.)

CARDO

Yeah, Ma? You need something?

TRUDY
> (TRUDY doesn't answer right away, adjusting the fabric with a critical eye.)

Can you come here for a minute?
> (CARDO enters the stage. He walks over to TRUDY, who's holding the blazer out to him.)

---

[3] An Afrikaans folk song.

                              TRUDY (cont.)
Get over here and try this on.
                    (CARDO slips on the blazer. TRUDY
                    stands, immediately fussing over him,
                    adjusting the shoulders, smoothing
                    the fabric, searching for flaws.)
No, No, These shoulders need work. They're too big. I can't have
you looking like you're drowning.

                              CARDO
Ma, why you still fussing? I look just like the other guys on the
team. What's the big deal?

                              TRUDY
The deal is it's my son's first parade. You step out right, or you
don't step at all.

                              CARDO
Don't you got better things to do? It's the holidays, Ma. Go
outside. Rest. Everybody else is enjoying it.

                              TRUDY
I enjoy keeping my hands busy. These fingers don't have much time
left in them, child. But while they still work, I'll make sure you
look right.

                              CARDO
The Jives aren't going to win Best Dressed, Ma. I'm sorry but we
never do. The Melody Makers take that trophy every year.

                              TRUDY
So what? Don't mean we can't still show up proper and look real
nice.
                    (fidgets with the blazer)
All those people gonna see you marching in the streets looking just
as fine as your daddy did back in his day. He wore his Jives outfit
with pride. It's like I can see him standing there.

                              CARDO
                    (looking offstage)
Ma, there's a car outside.

                              TRUDY
And? You see a car every day.

CARDO

Not like this one. It's...nice. Too nice for this street. Looks like some important fella behind the wheel too.

TRUDY

What kinda mischief you got into? In this neighbourhood, only the law comes knocking in a car like that.

CARDO

I haven't done anything. Honest! And, look, Mr. Solomons is with him, whoever he is. Here they come up the walk.

TRUDY

Go on, boy, answer the door. See what they want.

(CARDO walks to the edge of stage
right as ABE SOLOMONS and MR. WHITE
enter.)

ABE SOLOMONS
(to CARDO)
Don't you look like a showpiece!
(to MR. WHITE)
This here is Trudy's son, the Jolly Jives newest star.

CARDO

Uh, thanks, I guess.

ABE SOLOMONS

Your Ma around? Mind if we come in?

TRUDY

I'm right here, Abe. What's this about?

(CARDO leads them to TRUDY.)

ABE SOLOMONS

Trudy. Good to see you. Thought we'd stop by.

TRUDY

This time of year's got its way of bringing folks together, doesn't it?

(TRUDY gestures CARDO closer,
resuming her fitting.)

ABE SOLOMONS
Smells like something sweet in here. You've been baking?

TRUDY
Not this week.

ABE SOLOMONS
I was hoping you'd have some koesisters[4] ready. Been too long since I had yours.

TRUDY
If I got them, I'd give them. Family's been here, cleaning me out. There's none left. You want koesisters, go to the corner store.

ABE SOLOMONS
You know that's not a koesister. Anyway, you got a moment? We've got Mr. White here. He's from The Meridian.

MR. WHITE
How do you do? Hope you had yourself a nice Christmas.

TRUDY
Child, every Christmas is special when you're blessed enough to see it.
            (A brief pause. She looks MR. WHITE
            over, sizing him up quickly.)
So, what's The Meridian doing in my living room? And I thought old Ron was running things over there.

ABE SOLOMONS
Oh, that's right...nearly forgot how long you worked there, Trudy.

TRUDY
I gave them thirty good years. Sometimes it felt like I carried that whole place on my spine. All that bending and lifting left me with a back that creaks like an old door.

MR. WHITE
To answer your question, Ron retired years ago.

TRUDY
Now there's a man who knows how to run a place, and he could fold the corner of a bed like nobody's business.

---

[4] A traditional South African fried dough pastry, soaked in syrup, and coated with coconut.

MR. WHITE

I see, I see. Well, then if you worked for us, you know the calibre of guests we attract, Mrs. Trudy.

ABE SOLOMONS

Look Trudy, we're going around talking to all the troupe leaders about the...
> (looking at MR. WHITE)

...noise.

TRUDY

The noise?

MR. WHITE

The noise.
> (Another loud crash from outside interrupts the moment as the kids once again hit a ball against the window. MR. WHITE jumps, ducking behind the couch. TRUDY doesn't flinch.)

What in the—

TRUDY

Nobody's shooting at you, relax.
> (shouts off stage)

What did I tell you kids? Keep that ball outta my yard!
> (MR. WHITE hesitates, slowly peeking from behind the couch, trying to recover his composure.)

So, you complaining about noise, Mr. White?

MR. WHITE

A celebration, sure, I understand that. But It's a busy time for us, too, at 173 Central Boulevard. This year, we're hosting some very special guests. A Chinese millionaire, and the Russian ambassador. These people are here for a...peaceful escape.

TRUDY

And what's that mean for us, Mr. White? You want the Klopse[5] to parade like mice? Shuffle through without a sound?

MR. WHITE

I'm not asking you to be quiet, I'm just asking for a little consideration.

                              TRUDY
Well, sir, let me tell you, New Year's Day, that's for quiet. But
Tweede Nuwe Jaar? That's our day. It's not a parade if it doesn't
have the sounds, the cheers, the music. What do you think people
come out to see?

                            MR. WHITE
I don't mean any offence. I respect your tradition, but last year,
there were fights, trash everywhere—it looked like a...well, not
like a place I could invite the kind of guests we have this year.
It's...disruptive, and I don't think that's the impression you want
to give either, Mrs. Trudy.

                              TRUDY
I do apologise for all that, Mr. White. But those aren't my
Jolly Jivers. We run a respectable troupe.

                    (She adjusts the blazer's fit around
                    CARDO's chest, and he winces slightly.)

                          ABE SOLOMONS
Trudy, the Board's been talking. We're thinkin' maybe a different
route this year than Central Boulevard. Maybe we go down Hanover
Street.

                              TRUDY
You're sending us through the back alleys now? Tell me, Abe: what's
in this for you?

                          ABE SOLOMONS
The Meridian's been very generous to the Carnival this year.
Donations, you know. Could be...useful for the troupes.

                              TRUDY
Useful. Hmm. I'm listening.

                          ABE SOLOMONS
A food parcel or two, bus fare, school supplies for our kids...
things that help folks. Even Cardo. You know how expensive these
school rugby tournaments can be, Trudy. You can send him off without
begging for donations in the community.

                              CARDO
How much we talking, Mr. Solomons?

                          ABE SOLOMONS
Excuse me?

---

[5] Short for Kaapse Klopse (Cape Clubs), another name for the Cape Town Minstrel Carnival.

                              CARDO
How much is Mr. White giving us?

                          ABE SOLOMONS
Fifty thousand, if you must know.

                              CARDO
                      (to TRUDY)
I mean, it's not a big deal, Ma. It's just a street, right?

                              TRUDY
                      (to ABE SOLOMONS)
I'd walk to the ends of this city for my boy. I'd beg, I'd go
without. But I won't take bribe money for his future.

                              CARDO
Ow! Ma, you're pricking me!

                              TRUDY
Just hold still.

                          ABE SOLOMONS
Trudy...we're trying to be fair. That's why we're here, giving you
a heads-up. The board's already decided. We'll walk down Hanover
Street. This is just a courtesy.

                              TRUDY
We'll be on Central Boulevard, come Tweede Nuwe Jaar. Jolly Jives,
same as always. That's all I got to say.

                          ABE SOLOMONS
Trudy, if you go against the board, your troupe will be disbanded.
                      (TRUDY doesn't answer, focusing on
                      adjusting CARDO's collar, pulling
                      it snug against his neck. He winces
                      but stays silent. ABE SOLOMONS
                      exhales, nodding toward MR. WHITE.)
Thanks for letting us stop by.

                      (They move to the exit.)

                              TRUDY
Don't you remember, Abe?
                      (ABE SOLOMONS pauses midway to the
                      exit as the song "January, February,
                      March"[6] starts playing.)

---

[6] A traditional Cape Malay song.

TRUDY (cont.)
(The lights dim, and a soft spotlight
follows YOUNG TRUDY and YOUNG ABE
entering the stage. In this memory,
they are both decked out in their
bright Kaapse Klopse outfits. They
move in rhythm to the music as they
dance/walk across the stage down an
imaginary Central Boulevard. Their
painted faces smiling and laughing.
TRUDY speaks while their younger
selves perform.)

I know you remember what it was like, walking down Central
Boulevard. When we had nothing — not money, not much of a future.
But we marched. We had the sun on our backs, the sound of drums in
our bones. We marched with pride. When we were out there, walking
that street, it felt like the whole city was ours, remember that?
Folks hanging from balconies just to cheer us on. We had...a place,
if only for that one day.
(ABE SOLOMONS watches their younger
selves, caught between the past and
present, a bittersweet expression
on his face. The music fades, their
younger selves disappear off-stage,
the spotlight fades, and the stage
lights return to the present.)

ABE SOLOMONS
I remember.
(slight hesitation)
But that was then, Trudy. We're here now. And things change. Maybe
it's time. Maybe...you've done enough. Nobody's saying you gotta
keep this up.

MR. WHITE
I respect your pride in your troupe, Mrs. Trudy.
(They leave. A moment later,
MR. WHITE's voice can be heard
shouting off-stage to the unseen
kids outside.)
Watch where you're kicking that ball! My car's worth more than all
this!

TRUDY
(muttering to herself)
Next thing you know, they'll want to take the ground from under our
kids' feet, too.

                    CARDO
Why do you care so much about that route, Mama?

                    TRUDY
You wouldn't understand. Our people built those streets. But they
were never ours to walk on. Troupe members like your father put
their blood and tears into every step down that road, just for
the chance to walk it freely as a man of colour. Mr. White doesn't
know what he's asking. To kick us off Central Boulevard, it's like
taking something of your daddy's away.
                    (She steps back, taking in the full
                    picture of CARDO in the blazer. She
                    speaks, more to herself than to
                    CARDO.)
I think I've done enough. Take it off.

                    CARDO
You've done a lot, Ma. More than anyone else.
                    (CARDO removes the blazer,
                    carefully folding it.)

                    TRUDY
                    (smiling)
Come, I'll make us a fresh batch of koesisters. Pity that the
Russian ambassador will never know the rhythm of the Klopse and
hear what we hear when the drums beat.

                    (They start to move to the back of
                    the stage.)

                    CARDO
Maybe, but we'll make sure everyone else does.

                    (The lights dim as they continue
                    walking toward the back of the
                    stage.)

                    (BLACKOUT)

                    (END OF PLAY)

THE TAMALADA
————————————

A Play in One Act

by

Maya De La Torre

Cast of Characters

Aracelis: The middle child

Santiago: The youngest

Ama: The mother

Apa: The father

Luisa: The oldest and estranged

SCENE
Aracelis' kitchen

TIME
Present day

SETTING: ARACELIS' kitchen.

AT RISE: Darkness, except for a small sliver of
                                  light illuminating ARACELIS, who is
                                  kneeling in standard prayer position.

                              ARACELIS
Padre nuestro, que estás en el cielo. Santificado sea tu nombre.
...I do not remember the rest, I'm sorry. Please forgive me. You
know in my heart I know it. I'm just—okay, by that logic you also
know why I'm calling, or praying. Sorry. Feel free to strike me
down at any moment here. Lord knows you'd be doing me a favor...I'm
messing this up.
                    (rambling)
Padre   nuestro   que-estás-en-el-cielo-santificado-sea-tu-nombre-
venga-tu-reino-hágase-tu-voluntad-enlatierracomoenelcielo. Aha! I
remembered more! That's something, right? I feel at peace, so I'm
going with that's you telling me I did a good job.
                    (sobering up)
That's all I really want, God. I just want to do a good job. I
want—I've never done this before. I wasn't—that was Luisa. She's
the one who learned everything. She's the one that actually was
able to speak with Abuela. I can't, I just feel like there's a lot
riding on this, you know? Please don't let me burn any of the food.
Please let me hold my temper. Please make sure the surprise goes
well. Please make sure we all love each other by the end of this.
Please. Okay, I have to go. Merry Christmas. I mean, amen.

                    (ARACELIS finishes and turns around.
                    Lights on to reveal a kitchen in
                    chaos. Half a bag of masa is abandoned
                    in a bowl, the other half sits next
                    to another bag. A pot is practically
                    boiling over on the stove, full of
                    dried peppers. The corn husks are
                    soaking in a bowl of water on top of
                    some cookbooks. Vegetables are strewn
                    about, some half-peeled. Shopping
                    bags line the floor. The cherry on
                    top: SANTIAGO sitting on the counter
                    eating a concha.)

                              ARACELIS
What are you doing?

                        SANTIAGO
Pre-gaming.

                        ARACELIS
               (pushing him off counter)
You're disgusting, I make food here.
               (yanking concha from him)
Gimme that. You can't eat that. It's for the family.

                        SANTIAGO
I brought that from home—

                        ARACELIS
No, you didn't.

                        SANTIAGO
It's my travel pan dulce.
          (ARACELIS sets it down.)
Come on, let me have it.

                        ARACELIS
No.

                        SANTIAGO
No one's going to want it, it's half eaten.

                        ARACELIS
...that's true.

               (ARACELIS takes a bite.)

                        SANTIAGO
That's messed up. It's Christmas.

                        ARACELIS
Too bad...What are you doing here already? I thought you were
coming at four with everyone else.

                        SANTIAGO
I was in the area.

                        ARACELIS
You go to college two hours away.

                        SANTIAGO
...I, uh, yeah, I wanted to see if you needed any help.

                    ARACELIS
            (shocked)
What?

                    SANTIAGO
Don't—don't make a big deal out of it, I just—

                    ARACELIS
            (hugging him)
Sonny...

                    SANTIAGO
            (accepting it)
Shut up.

                    ARACELIS
Can you check the peppers?

                    SANTIAGO
Yeah.
            (opening the pot)
Jesus Christ.

                    ARACELIS
What?

                    SANTIAGO
            (coughing)
I think you made a bomb.

                    ARACELIS
Good, that means it's good.

                    SANTIAGO
Put your face in this.

                    ARACELIS
Absolutely not.
            (getting the blender out)
Put those in here.

                    SANTIAGO
            (doing it)
Why didn't you just buy the chile?

                         ARACELIS
                    (puts lard into the masa)
Mom likes it more like that. Put salt in that.

                         SANTIAGO
                    (doing it)
Actually, once you get past getting maced in the face, it smells
pretty good.

                         ARACELIS
Thanks.
                    (As SANTIAGO starts the blender)
Do you think Luisa will show up?

                         SANTIAGO
                    (stopping blender)
What?

                         ARACELIS
Nothing.
                    (SANTIAGO starting blender)
I don't even know if I want her to come or not. I mean I do, I
invited her, and I want her to come, but—

                         SANTIAGO
                    (stopping blender)
Aracelis. Pick better times to talk. What is going on?

                         ARACELIS
Luisa.

                         SANTIAGO
Oh...What about her?

                         ARACELIS
She's coming.

                         SANTIAGO
Today?

                         ARACELIS
Yeah.

                         SANTIAGO
Shit.

                        ARACELIS
Yeah.

                        SANTIAGO
Does Mom know?

                        ARACELIS
No.

                        SANTIAGO
Shit...This chile better be good.

                        ARACELIS
It's Abuelita's recipe.

                        SANTIAGO
                (bringing chile to the masa)
Should I just pour this in there?

                        ARACELIS
Not this one.
                (dumping a other bag into another
                bowl)
This one.
                (SANTIAGO pours the chile into the
                new bowl and starts to mix it.)
Taste this.
                (SANTIAGO does.)
More salt?

                        SANTIAGO
No, that's good.
                (ARACELIS covers the masa with saran
                wrap and puts away empty grocery
                bags.)
She said she was going to come?

                        ARACELIS
She did. But I guess you don't really know with her...I'm really
nervous.

                        SANTIAGO
You made homemade chile. You're resurrecting a long lost tradition
we haven't done since Abuelita died.

                              ARACELIS
I'm doing that because I'm scared I'm about to blow everything up,
so it's not even a pure intention. It's infected with ulterior
motives.

                              SANTIAGO
You're so dramatic.

                              ARACELIS
I just miss her.

                              SANTIAGO
...I miss her too.

                    (They continue in silence. SANTIAGO
                    tries to give ARACELIS a taste from
                    his finger.)

                              ARACELIS
Gross.
                    (He wipes the masa on his hands onto
                    a spoon and gives it to ARACELIS. She
                    hesitates, then eats it.)
A little more.
                    (He adds a bit more. She tries it.)
Perfect.
                    (He washes his hands as ARACELIS
                    covers the food. The doorbell rings.)
Shit, shit, shit.

                              SANTIAGO
Gogogogo. I'll clean up. Go.

                    (ARACELIS straightens her apron and
                    wipes her hands. She fixes her hair and
                    exits. Back on stage, SANTIAGO hides
                    some pots in the cabinet. Offstage,
                    the sound of a family reuniting.
                    SANTIAGO poses "naturally." AMA and
                    APA enter with ARACELIS.)

                              AMA
Mija, it smells so good in here.

                              ARACELIS
Thank you Ama.

                         APA
                (going to hug SANTIAGO)
They teach you how to cook in college?

                      SANTIAGO
A little.

                         AMA
                (giving SANTIAGO a squeeze)
Mijo. Your hair is too long.

                         APA
                (whispering)
He likes it like that.

                         AMA
                (whispering)
It's in his eyes.

                      SANTIAGO
I can hear you.

                         AMA
Shhh, amor. What can we do?

                      ARACELIS
Nothing. We're just about ready-

                (A knock at the door. AMA and APA
                look around.)

                         AMA
Who is that?

                      ARACELIS
The neighbor, I don't know. I'll be right back.

                (ARACELIS, panicked, gestures toward
                SANTIAGO, then exits.)

                      SANTIAGO
So...anyone want some pan dulce?

                         APA
Mijo, how are your estudios?

                    SANTIAGO
So wine then? Vodka?

                    AMA
Sonny!

          (ARACELIS re-enters with LUISA.
          There's silence.)

                    LUISA
I should go.

                    ARACELIS
No, Luisa.

                    LUISA
No, this was a bad idea. I'm—

                    AMA
          (softly)
Isa...

                    LUISA
          (crying)
Ama.

          (They hug with tears and apologies.
          APA stands off, but is pulled into
          the hug too. SANTIAGO and ARACELIS
          watch. A long moment.)

                    LUISA
          (laughing)
Are we eating tamales?

                    ARACELIS
Yes!

               (BLACKOUT)

               (END OF PLAY)

FIVE GOLDEN RINGS

_____

A Play in One Act

by

Louis DeVaughn Nelson

Cast of Characters

Marla:	Female, 20s. The youngest and most mature out of the family. Pregnant. Libra.
Melinda:	Female, 40s. Marla's mother. Spoiled princess. Talented photographer. Virgo.
Aaron:	Male, 50s. Mr. Melinda. Golden Retriever vibes. Taurus.
Mary Anne:	Female, 60s. Melinda's mother. Easy going and a little sassy. Sagittarius.
Clyde:	Male, 60s. Mr. Mary Anne. Debonair and a little jaded. Scorpio.

SCENE
A public park, United States

TIME
2024, around the holidays

SETTING: A public park. Trees are upstage in the
                                  background. There is a wooden picnic table
                                  downstage.

AT RISE: Lights up on a wooden picnic table right
                                  where MARLA sits, a fashionable Gen Z'er
                                  doing all the things on her phone. The
                                  picnic table is littered with photography
                                  equipment, flanked by some haphazard drinks
                                  and snacks snagged at the local gas station
                                  right before their arrival. There's
                                  also a large picture frame standing up
                                  against the table. MELINDA, a geriatric
                                  millennial, is taking some test shots of
                                  her mother, the 60-going-on-20 year old,
                                  MARY ANNE who is absolutely eating every
                                  pose.)

                          MELINDA
That's good mom. Yup. Good. Hold it there. Yes. Very nice.

                  (CLYDE strolls in from stage left
                  with a beer, crossing in front of
                  the shot.)

                          MARY ANNE
Excuse you.

                          MELINDA
Dad!

                          CLYDE
My fault, my fault. I thought y'all was still practicing.

                          MELINDA
We are, but—

                          MARY ANNE
Let's be honest, I probably got it on the first shot.

                  (MARY ANNE approaches the camera to
                  review her work with MELINDA. CLYDE
                  sits behind MARLA.)

                          MARLA
I don't think you can drink that out here, pop-pop.

                    CLYDE
Whaddu mean? We outside.

                    MARLA
You didn't see that big sign at the entrance to the park? No, this.
No, that. No, everything.

                    CLYDE
I went to war for this country, I think I get a pass.

                    MARLA
I think you're right.

                    MELINDA
            (to MARLA)
Marla baby, can you hand me one of them new cards? I think we're
good to go. I wanna catch this light before them clouds get over
here.

            (MARLA obliges and MARY ANNE checks
             her makeup.)

                    MARLA
You look sick grandma.

                    MARY ANNE
Oh, my god! What do you mean?

                    MARLA
No, like good. Like fierce, like really pretty.

                    MARY ANNE
Oh, thank you sweetie. And don't call me grandma. We already went
over this too many times. I'm not quite ready for that title yet.
Just call me May May.

                    CLYDE
Mary Anne, you have always been quite a handful.

                    MARY ANNE
            (falling into CLYDE's lap)
I know, that's why you love me.

                    CLYDE
One of about a million reasons.

MARY ANNE

Oh, Clyde! Start!

> (They go at it to MARLA's chagrin. She
> looks at her phone. MELINDA crosses
> over.)

MELINDA

I wonder what my lovely husband is getting into. He's usually much more attentive than this. Lately he's been kind of...

MARLA

I think he's getting the rest of the snacks out of the car.

MELINDA

Let me show you how to work this camera so you can get some shots of me.

MARLA

Why can't I use my phone?

MELINDA

Because, I have to edit all of us into one shot.

MARLA

What are you talking about, you have a tripod.

MELINDA

Oh, no! I didn't show you? I want to do that picture frame thing that's trending on TikTok. I thought I told you.

MARLA

What trend?

MELINDA

You spend literally every second on that app, how have you not seen it?

MARLA

Actually, I don't—

MELINDA

Well, aren't you an influencer, and you make all this money, allegedly?

CLYDE

Melinda.

                              MARLA
What do you mean allegedly?

                             MELINDA
I'm just saying, once the baby's born you're gonna have to start—

                              MARLA
I'm gonna have to start what? Not you trying to be a mother all of
a sudden.

                              CLYDE
Marla.

                             MELINDA
You know what. This happens every year. I try to do something nice
to bring the family together and—

                            MARY ANNE
Ah, here she goes.

                    (AARON, MELINDA's smiley and sloppy
                    husband, stumbles in from stage
                    left. He spills a bag of snacks.)

                             MELINDA
All I wanted to do was take these cute photos, of all of us, in
these little frames, all four generations of Taylors, strong Taylor
women. I just wanted to create this space like I do every year—every
year without anybody's help. I do it all by myself. You all don't
have to do nothing, and I get us together so we can make another
nice friendly fun Christmas card and send them out to everyone and
remember our love for each other because the world is just so crazy
right now and the planet is melting and we're all gonna...

                              AARON
Ah! whoopsie daisies!

                            MARY ANNE
Perfect timing Aaron, once again.

                              MARLA
Did you just say, "whoopsie daisies"?

                    (MARLA and MARY ANNE help AARON.
                    CLYDE comforts MELINDA.)

                         CLYDE
Relax. Relate. Release. Relax. Relate. Release.

                    CLYDE and MELINDA
                       (in unison)
Relax. Relate. Release. Relax. Relate. Release.

                         AARON
You okay, honey bunny?

                        MELINDA
                      (facetious)
I'm very relaxed, per usual.

                         AARON
                   (affectionately)
Of course. I'd expect nothing less.

                        MELINDA
What took you so long?

                         AARON
The snacks. I have one more bag.

                        MELINDA
But we're going to spoil our dinner.

                         AARON
I thought this was dinner.

                        MELINDA
Aaron! Look at all this junk.

                         AARON
I'm sorry. I'm sorry. Look—I got Kombucha! Anything you want me
to go get? It'll only take a minute.

                        MELINDA
No, just get the rest of the stuff. Hurry up, you took so long the
last time.

                         AARON
I was just checking the oil and making sure the tire pressure was
okay.
                         CLYDE
You didn't have to do that.

                              MELINDA
Yes, he did. It's his thing.

                              AARON
I'll go get the rest. I don't want it to go to waste.

                              MARLA
Don't worry, Dad. Whatever we don't eat I'll take over to the
community fridge.

                              MELINDA
You sure you don't want to take it home?

                              MARLA
Yeah, I'm sure.

                              MELINDA
Well, okay. I guess if you're just so fully stocked all the time
and everything.

                              MARLA
I have plenty to eat at home, Mom. Do you think I don't?

                              AARON
We know you have plenty, we just want you to know that we're here
if you need us.

                              MARLA
Oh, so she's been getting in your ear about my job status.

                              AARON
Well, you do social media. And soon you're going to be a mom, and
like, we just want you to know you don't need to have a backup plan.
You have us.

                              MARLA
But—

                              MELINDA
It's fine, child. So what we spent half a fortune on you getting
your MBA. Obviously it's too late to put that to good use. You can
coast a little bit, once again, for a little while, and then you
can go back and do your little social media thing once the baby
gets a little older.

MARLA

Excuse me? My "little social media thing"? You guys know I make twice as much as both of you, combined.

AARON

It's not all about money, Marla.

MARLA

I can support myself, and I can support my baby.

MELINDA

Here you go again, always pushing us away. Just like you do with every man who ever—

CLYDE

Melinda.

MARLA

Oh, no. Not the unmarried mother thing again.

MELINDA

What happened to Carlos? He was perfect!

MARLA

I'm sorry that I haven't become the spitting image of you and followed all the dreams you missed out on and became the complacent corporate slave you wanted me to be, but believe it or not, I'm happy and healthy, and that's all I'm going to want for my child. No more, no less.

MELINDA

Well, I—

MARY ANNE

Weren't y'all talking about getting pictures with this light? I mean, I'm beautiful either way, but let's get this show on the road please.

AARON
(while exiting)
I'm going to go get the rest of the food.

MARLA
(looking at her phone)
I found the trend online. It is really cute. So we each have to pose with the frame in front of us, and then we can just layer each photo within the frame. I can do it on my app if you want.

                    MELINDA
Well, I mean, you're the professional, so...

                    MARLA
You're a professional too, Mom. I'm just trying to work smarter,
not harder. Don't worry, my phone is pretty high res.

                    MARY ANNE
Alright, let's try it.
          (to CLYDE)
Tell me I'm gorgeous.

                    CLYDE
The most beautiful, glorious, luminescent beast I've ever laid
eyes on.

          (MARY ANNE grabs the picture frame and
          goes off to pose with it, spritely,
          sultry.)

                    MELINDA
Have y'all noticed anything different about Aaron?

                    MARY ANNE
Well, he's lost quite a bit of weight after he dabbled with ozempic.

                    MELINDA
Did you notice he wasn't wearing his ring?
          (MARY ANNE deflates.)

                    MARLA
What?

                    MELINDA
He went to some conference in Seattle last month and he hasn't worn
it since, and I asked him about it, and he said he's been having
issues with retaining water or something, and he was thinking
about getting a new one, but he hasn't planned a trip for us to
go shopping together to look. Every time I look at him all I can
see is that blank space on his finger, and he looks naked, but not
in the good way. In the bad way—the really, really bad way—and
I think there's somebody else. I mean, there has to be somebody
else because he's always so chipper and eager to please, and he's
so reassuring and passionate that it can only mean he doesn't love
me and he's met someone better than me that he loves more than me,

MELINDA (cont.)

and I don't want to end up on Dateline NBC where everyone says she lit up every room she ever entered after I'm murdered and stashed in some weird, stupid place because your father, he's smart, but he's not smart smart all the time, and I—

CLYDE

Relax. Relate. Release.

MARLA and CLYDE
                (in unison)
Relax. Relate. Release.

ALL
                (in unison)
Relax. Relate. Release. Relax. Relate. Release.

MARLA

Mom, I've never seen anybody love on somebody as hard as Dad loves on you.
                (to EVERYONE)
Present company excluded. It's just a ring. What you have can't be boiled down to a ring. It's just a symbol.

MELINDA

Do you hate that I want that for you some day too?

MARLA

No, Mom, I don't hate it. I just think—we're different. And that's okay.

MELINDA

I know sweetie, it's just that motherhood is a lovely thing to share.

MARLA

I'm sharing it with the people I love, don't worry.

MELINDA

Worrying is my thing. I'm a mom. You'll see!

MARLA

I know.

MARY ANNE

Can I ask you a question, dear child of mine?

                        MELINDA
Shoot.

                        MARY ANNE
Why are we making a Christmas card this year? Didn't you convert
to Judaism for your little husband?

                        MELINDA
Well, yes. And please don't call him "little husband". We're very
much in love!

                        MARLA
It's a holiday card.

                        MARY ANNE
It's so funny what you kids will do for a man these days. I only
have to do one thing. Ain't that right babycakes?

          (MARY ANNE blows a kiss to CLYDE. He
          catches.)

                        MARLA
Okay, enough. Let's do both versions and see what happens.

                        MELINDA
Sounds good.

          (MARY ANNE poses. MARLA and MELINDA
          snap and compare photos. AARON enters
          with a gift bag.)

                        CLYDE
There he is.

                        MELINDA
Where are the rest of the groceries?

                        AARON
I got a little surprise. Everyone gather around.

                        MELINDA
What's this about?

                        AARON
Relax, relate, release my darling. It's good news. I got a little
box for you.

(AARON offers MELINDA the box.
Bright reactions all around.)

MELINDA

What is this? What are you doing?

AARON

I lost my ring when I went to Seattle. A horrible hair gel incident.
I know you've noticed, and I was too embarrassed to talk about it.
But I got another one, and another one for you. But it's for your
ring finger on the other hand. I know you've been going through a
lot lately, doing all the stuff with the conversion for me, for us.
And I want to renew our vows.

MELINDA

This can't be real.

AARON
        (kneeling)
Would you do me the honor of marrying me, again?

MELINDA

Well, yes!
            (They kiss. Some applause. Some
            tears.)
This is so ridiculous. Wait, what else is in the bag?

AARON

Well, early Christmas gifts, I guess? I got rings for everyone! Like
in the song. *Five Golden Rings*. See, I can be Christian sometimes!

(AARON hands them out.)

MARLA

Dad, what is actually wrong with you?

MARY ANNE

So y'all don't celebrate Hanukkah anymore? I'm confused.

MELINDA

We're doing a combo of both, Mom.

MARY ANNE

I was hoping I was going to get a different present every night of
the week. But I know that's not what it's all about.

                         MELINDA
For every Jewish person, there's a different way to be Jewish, just
so you know.

                        MARY ANNE
                   (admiring her ring)
Ooohhh, I might have to convert myself. Nice choice dear son-in-
law.

                         CLYDE
Yes, thank you Aaron, this is a nice gesture.

                         AARON
                   (to MARLA)
Don't make this weird. It's not symbolic or anything, just a
special treat for my little girl. I can't believe how fast you've
grown up!

                         MARLA

Thanks daddy.

                         MELINDA
Ok, the clouds are coming back. Let's get a family shot while the
feelings are fresh and untainted!

                    (They all gather as MELINDA sets up
                    a tripod shot. She sets the timer.
                    They pose. Photos snap. MARLA takes
                    out her phone and gets a selfie of
                    everyone.)

                    (BLACKOUT)

                    (END OF PLAY)

THE PRINCIPLE OF THE MATTER

A Play in One Act

by

Russell Nichols

Cast of Characters

Kujichagulia:	Assertive yet guarded with a bone-dry sarcasm. She takes decisive action, but struggles in groups. Represents self-determination.
Ujima:	Team player and awkward people-pleaser. He works hard, especially to impress his crush, Kuji. Represents collective work and responsibility.
Ujamaa:	An ambitious entrepreneur juggling various ventures. He wants to deliver his people to financial freedom. Represents cooperative economics.
Nia:	Morally principled and rigid. As the group's compass, she keeps others on course, verging on neuroticism. Represents purpose.
Kuumba:	Dramatically artsy and fashionably risky. She yearns for the space to express herself loudly and freely. Represents creativity.
Imani:	Sensitive yet strong, she possesses an optimistic spirit and her soft-spoken kindness is often mistaken for weakness. Represents faith.

SCENE
Community center

TIME
The day after Christmas

SETTING: A community center. A bedrock in the
                                  neighborhood, always booked for some
                                  celebration.

AT RISE: Lights up on remnants of Christmas chaos
                                  from a party last night scattered all
                                  over the place. A bare table sits in the
                                  middle. NIA enters, huffing while hauling
                                  a bloated bag over her shoulder.

                        NIA
Oh, I don't believe this.
                (She nearly drops the bag at the filthy
                sight before her. Calling back.)
Kuji, come look at this mess!

                        KUJICHAGULIA
                (rushing in with another bag)
What you hollering like that for, Nia?

                        NIA
Will you look at this mess.

                        KUJICHAGULIA
I'm looking.

                        NIA
Can you believe this?

                        KUJICHAGULIA
Not looking too good.

                        NIA
How are we supposed to celebrate in here?

                        KUJICHAGULIA
I thought Umoja was on clean-up duty.

                        NIA
Lemme call him.

                        KUJICHAGULIA
Call him, girl.

                (NIA calls. As the phone rings...and
                rings. KUJI sets up the table with
                the African cloth and mkeka.)

                              NIA
His mailbox is full.

                         KUJICHAGULIA
And I know what it's full of.

                              NIA
                    (unpacking the mazao/fruits)
We had an agreement.

                         KUJICHAGULIA
Mm-mm, see, I don't agree with agreements. If you want something
done, you know what you gotta do.

                              NIA
Kuji, I can't do everything myself.

                         KUJICHAGULIA
                    (unpacking the muhindi/corn)
It's an acquired taste.

                              NIA
                    (unpacking the kikombe cha umoja/
                    unity cup)
We need to rely on each other.

                         KUJICHAGULIA
Not I. No, ma'am. I'm Kujichagulia and I work for the DIY...wait,
wait, please tell me you got the candles.

                              NIA
Umoja—

                         KUJICHAGULIA
Don't tell me that.

                              NIA
He was supposed to clean up and leave the kinara with the candles
here last night. That was the agreement.

                         KUJICHAGULIA
Your little agreement's on a red-eye to a big disagreement.

                              NIA
                    (sitting to gather herself)
What are we gonna do?

                         KUJICHAGULIA
              (repacking)
There's always next time.

                              NIA
They'll be here any minute!

                         KUJICHAGULIA
Tell 'em I said whassup.

                              NIA
What's Kwanzaa without candles?

                         KUJICHAGULIA
Poorly lit.

                              NIA
              (tapping her palms quickly,
              trapped between laughing and
              completely losing it)
How...how...this isn't...no, I-I can't...I can't. What is this? I
don't...we have the mkeka and the mazao and the muhindi and we have
the kikombe cha umoja!

                         KUJICHAGULIA
You mad?

                              NIA
I'm...I'm not mad. I'm disappointed.

                         KUJICHAGULIA
              (sighs and begrudgingly unpacks the
              fruit)
Listen, it's the end of the year, not the end of the world. We'll
handle it. I'll handle it. I can grab some candles from the corner
store, no problem.
              (unpacks the corn)
These jokers prolly won't be here for another hour anyway. You know
how we be—

              (Right then, IMANI enters.)

                              IMANI
Habari gani, family? And remind me to never play designated driver
again.

                              NIA
What? Who was drinking?

                              IMANI
Frick and Frack. Off that get-rich-quick Kool-Aid.

                    (UJIMA and UJAMAA enter, talking
                    money a mile-a-minute.)

                              UJAMAA
...because the money's right there, fam.

                              UJIMA
Right in front of us.

                              UJAMAA
That's what I'm saying.

                              UJIMA
It's going to somebody.

                              UJAMAA
Why not us?

                              UJIMA
We know why.
                    (The friends carry on.)

        IMANI   UJAMAA
    (to NIA and KUJI)   (to UJIMA)
    Imagine being stuck   I'm talking billions
    in holiday traffic with   in grants. All that
    this ringing in your   fundage. Just sitting
    ear.   right there.

        KUJICHAGULIA   UJIMA
    I don't want to.   And if they don't get
                                    used in a year, what
                                    happens?

        IMANI   UJAMAA
    It's worse than Bruce   The funds expire like
    Springsteen's "Santa   spoiled milk. Glug,
    Claus is Coming to Town."   glug! Down the drain.

        NIA   UJIMA
    Where's Kuumba?   Straight up wasted.

IMANI
After that ride, she
needed to "recharge."
But we're all here now,
so everything will be
alright.

UJAMAA
Like that grant money
could be distributed
accordingly, you feel
what I'm saying? I mean,
they owe us. That's
reparations.

KUJICHAGULIA
Is that right?

UJIMA
Compensation.

IMANI
Except I wasn't able to
reach Umoja...

UJAMAA
Remuneration.

UJIMA
Consternation.

(UJAMAA grimaces at UJIMA, then
backs away to greet NIA and KUJI.)

UJAMAA
Umoja? Where he at? I loaned him fifty buckers to buy a
kinara and some candles.

(UJIMA greets them too, but gives
an awkward sorta-kinda hug to his
secret crush, KUJI.)

KUJICHAGULIA
Wait, Ujamaa, you paid for the candles?

UJAMAA
No, no, I gave him a loan to buy the candles.

IMANI
Where's the unity cup?

(KUJI unpacks the cup as UJIMA holds
out his hand.)

UJIMA
Oh, allow me to help you with that, queen—
                (KUJI sets the cup on the table.)
You got it. I'll, uh...I'll clean up all this Christmas junk then.
You wanna help me out, Ujamaa?

                    UJAMAA
What I want is my fifty buckers.

          (UJAMAA and UJIMA push the clutter
          into separate piles.)

                    IMANI
Wasn't Umoja supposed to take care of that?

          (They shrug.)

                    NIA
          (NIA climbs up on the chair,
          raising her hands.)
Attention everyone! I have something important to say—

          (Right then, conga drums rumble from
          somewhere. Everybody turns. KUUMBA
          bursts in, banging away, launching
          into an impromptu dance/spoken word
          number.)

                    KUUMBA
'Twas the day after Christmas / All through the community / We
standing on business / To celebrate unity like—
          (a la Queen Latifah)
U.N.I.T.Y.! U.N.I.T ...
          (KUUMBA trails off.)
Who died?

                    KUJICHAGULIA
Your stylist, apparently.

                    UJAMAA
What's the deal, Nia?

                    UJIMA
Is there something we can help with?

                    NIA
Alright, everybody, here's the situation: We're here to celebrate
the first day of Kwanzaa, but there's been a critical oversight that
must first be rectified to honor the integrity of this—

                    KUJICHAGULIA
Umoja's missing.

                        KUUMBA
Missing?

              (A wave of confusion washes over the
              room—frowns, uncertain smiles.)

                        UJIMA
Ha! That's a good one. You almost got us—

                        KUJICHAGULIA
And we got no candles.

                        UJAMAA
Whoa, whoa, what?

                        KUJICHAGULIA
And Nia's mad about it.

                        NIA
I'm not mad—

                        KUJICHAGULIA
My bad. "Disappointed." Because we got no candles.

                        UJAMAA
I'm mad too!

                        NIA
It's not about the candles, it's the principle of the
matter. We had an agreement—

                        KUJICHAGULIA
—that he reneged on.

                        UJIMA
But where's Umoja at though?

                        KUUMBA
What if he's in trouble?

                        UJAMAA
If he's not, he will be.

                        KUUMBA
Maybe he forgot.

                              NIA
To show up? We do this every year.

                              UJIMA
Umoja never misses a party.

                              IMANI
He'll be here. Trust me. He's running late, probably stuck in
holiday traffic, but he'll be here. Have a little faith.

                         KUJICHAGULIA
I'm allergic.

                              UJIMA
This is nuts! We should just call him!

                              NIA
Tried that. He didn't answer. And his mailbox is full.

                              UJAMAA
Kuumba, you call.

                              KUUMBA
Moi?

                              UJAMAA
He's...interested in you.

                              KUUMBA
                    (blushing)
Is that so?

                         KUJICHAGULIA
Girl, you can do better.

                              KUUMBA
                    (KUUMBA calls. The phone rings and
                    rings. The room falls silent. KUUMBA
                    looks dejected.)
His mailbox is full...who was the last person to speak with Umoja?

                              UJAMAA
He asked me to borrow fifty buckers the day before yesterday.

                              UJIMA
He texted me Christmas morning asking where to buy a kinara.

                         NIA
He called me last night.
                    (Everybody turns to NIA. She steps
                    down from the chair.)
His family rented this place out for their Christmas party. He
promised me he'd clean up and leave the candles here. Then go home,
change, and come back to celebrate with us.

                        IMANI
And any second now...
               (pointing off)
...he'll walk through that door.

                    (Everybody turns to look offstage.
                    Nobody   walks   through   the   door.
                    Everybody side-eyes IMANI.)

        KUJICHAGULIA   UJIMA
    Never trust a psychic.   How irresponsible!

            KUUMBA   UJAMAA
      Is he ghosting me?   That's called phantom
                                       debt.

                        NIA
People, please, let's focus on the principle at hand—

                        IMANI
I concur.

                        NIA
               (rushing around the table, holding
               up items)
Nobody knows where Umoja is. We have no kinara and no candles, but
what do we have? We got the kente cloth. We got the mkeka. Right?
We have the mazao, which represent what?

                        IMANI
The harvest!

                        NIA
And the muhindi, which represents what now?

            IMANI   UJIMA
        (nudging UJIMA)   (annoyed)
        The children!   ...the children.

                    UJAMAA
Which one represents my fifty buckers?

                    NIA
And the kikombe cha umoja, which represents what?

                    IMANI
Unity!

                    KUUMBA
          (banging on the drums again, launching
          into her impromptu dance/spoken word
          number)
'Twas the day after Christmas / All through the community / We
standing on business / To celebrate—hold up.
          (KUUMBA pauses, putting backhand
          to forehead. IMANI, deflated, stops
          dancing.)
I shan't go on.

                    NIA
What's wrong?

                    UJAMAA
Drama queen.

                    KUUMBA
How can one's artistry shine in such darkness?

                    UJIMA
It's bright in here.

                    KUJICHAGULIA
Evidently not.

                    IMANI
C'mon, Kuumba, you got this!

                    KUUMBA
I'm not to perform until after the match strikes and we light the
first candle, illuminating my movements in the incandescent glow of
that sacred flame.

                    KUJICHAGULIA
Sounds like hell.

(IMANI runs to cut off the lights.
In the dark, she rushes back, breaks
out her cell and shines the light on
KUUMBA's face.)

IMANI
Look, you're glowing, beloved. Now, c'mon, keep it going—
(a la Queen Latifah)
U.N.I.T.Y.! C'mon everybody! U.N.I.T.Y.!
(Still, nobody feels it.)
Am I alone here?

(An awkward silence and mumbled
affirmatives.)

UJIMA
(turning on lights)
Yo sis, I'm with you, but Kuumba's right. I mean, I just can't
call it Kwanzaa without the kinara—

NIA
What can you call it, then?

KUJICHAGULIA
How 'bout we call it a night.

NIA
No! We're not calling it a night. We're here to celebrate the first
day of—

UJIMA
We can't celebrate Umoja without Umoja!

IMANI
He will be here.

KUJICHAGULIA
(to IMANI)
Somebody's had too much egg nog.

KUUMBA
What about my grand performance?!

UJAMAA
Why don't we write off Umoja and start with Kujichagulia?

                    KUJICHAGULIA
Now you're speaking my language.

                        UJIMA
I can get behind that—

                         NIA
No, no, no! You can't just skip days all willy-nilly! There's an
order to this—a proper...functional protocol that honors the
spirit of our ancestors.

          (A moment of silence.)

                       KUUMBA
Why don't we ask them where Umoja's hiding?

                        UJIMA
Yeah, you go 'head and do that, Kuumba. And in the meantime, I say
we sit down and collectively brainstorm how to celebrate Kwanzaa
without a kinara and candles.

                         NIA
Ujima, that's what I'm talking about! That's a plan.
                    (UJIMA beams until KUJI groans. UJIMA
                    winces. The group unfolds chairs,
                    then slumps down in a circle.)
Now, who wants to go first?

                       UJAMAA
According to "order," Umoja is supposed to go first, so—

                         NIA
You know what I meant, Ujamaa, but since you volunteered to open
your big mouth, let's hear your big idea.

                       UJAMAA
My idea? For a kinara?
              (then: an epiphany)
I propose a fundraiser.

                    KUJICHAGULIA
That's not fun.

                       UJAMAA
We each donate ten dollars to the pot, then I'll go out and buy a
kinara set right quick. Boom. Problem solved.

                         IMANI
What happens to the extra ten, beloved?

                        KUUMBA
If each of us contributes ten, that makes sixty. So if the kinara
set costs only fifty, what becomes of the profit?

                        UJAMAA
Goes in my pocket. That's called a delivery fee.

                     KUJICHAGULIA
That's called rob-ber-y.

                        UJAMAA
You always talking, Kuji! I don't hear you saying nothing.

               (KUJI cocks her head at the
               absurdity of the statement.)

                         UJIMA
Everyone, just calm down.

                         IMANI
Let's all take a deep breath.

                        KUUMBA
Indeed, this negative energy is disturbing the muse.

                     KUJICHAGULIA
               (stands, confrontational)
Nah, nah, I wanna hear what the pyramid schemer has to say.

                          NIA
Kuji, don't—

                     KUJICHAGULIA
The man who puts the broke in real estate broker.

                        UJAMAA
At least I'm out here tryna do something for the people. You only
think about yourself, you self-centered sadist!

               (The room goes quiet, thick with
               butter knife-type tension.)

                         KUJICHAGULIA
                (nodding and pacing around them with
                      hands behind her)
I think about other things.

                            UJIMA
Really? Like what?

                         KUJICHAGULIA
Why am I here?

                            IMANI
Mmmmmmm. Existentially?

                         KUJICHAGULIA
Literally.

                            IMANI
I feel that.

                         KUJICHAGULIA
Why am I here in this group? What's the purpose?

                             NIA
To celebrate—

                         KUJICHAGULIA
Uh-uh, I don't wanna hear that.
                (moves behind the table)
We do the same thing year after year after year. We light candles,
we bring gifts, we "Harambee!" But to what end? What are we
celebrating? I mean, look the hell around.
                (they look around)
What are we actually celebrating?
                (re: the fruits)
The harvest is burning.
                (re: the corn)
The children are dying.
                (re: the cup)
And unity? I don't know. Maybe I am a sadist. But if I am, we all
are...which is why I'm leaving the group.

                            UJIMA
What?!

                            KUUMBA
You mustn't!

                          NIA
Kuji, you're a vital part of this—

                     KUJICHAGULIA
What? This Reading Rainbow Coalition? Whatever we are, it doesn't
matter.

                         IMANI
Oh, don't say that. You have to hold on, Kujichagulia.

                     KUJICHAGULIA
Imani, I don't have what you have. I don't wake up every day
feeling all happy and hopeful. That...that ain't me.

                        UJAMAA
But that's why we're here, sis. To invest in each other.

                     KUJICHAGULIA
               (KUJI takes this in. Then laughs,
               shaking her head.)
This is a mess. We're a mess. You can't invest in mess, so with
that said, I wish you all a Happy Kwanzaa! I'm out.

               (KUJI heads out.)

                          NIA
Kuji, you have to stay.

                     KUJICHAGULIA
Why should I?

                         UJIMA
               (bolts up)
Because I'm in love with you!
               (Everybody turns to UJIMA, shocked
               by the confession, including KUJI,
               who freezes at the exit. UJIMA is
               flustered.)
I mean, we all are. We need you, Kuji. You're strong and decisive
and assertive. You inspire us—you inspire me. And if you leave,
then...then I'm leaving too!

               (Reluctantly, UJIMA heads for the
               exit, emboldened by each step.)

                        KUUMBA
                  (banging on her drum)
And the muse is calling me to express myself elsewhere!

                  (KUUMBA heads for the exit.)

                        UJAMAA
And I could use a ride, so I'ma roll out with y'all.

                  (UJAMAA heads for the exit.)

                        NIA
                  (head in hands)
I don't believe this—

                        IMANI
That's the damn problem!
                  (Everybody turns around.)
That's why we're in this situation now. We stopped believing! We
stopped believing in ourselves. In each other. In the ones who came
before us.
                  (empathetic)
I understand it's hard to hold on when you everything looks bleak.
I don't wake up happy and hopeful every day. Some days, I wake up
hurting. Some days I wish I didn't wake up at all. I know how that
feels. I know the agony of losing hope, of losing my head, of losing
someone I love...I know how scary it is to move forward when you
can't see what's ahead.But this is what the mission calls for! This
is how we survive, how we've always survived! How we got over! As
we try and try again to find our way in the dark, we have to hold
on to each other...
                  (hand to heart)
And it breaks my heart when I hear somebody say this doesn't matter.
Matter is anything that occupies space, and we're standing here,
together, occupying this space. Each with something special to
bring to the table: Kuumba with your creative expression; Nia with
your purposefulness; Ujamaa with your plans for building communal
wealth; Ujima with your powerful work ethic; Kujichagulia with your
dedication to taking action. We all matter. And yes, it might be a
mess, but if we work together, we can clean it up.
                  (raising fist)
Now, who's with me?

                  (A long silence.)

KUJICHAGULIA

Good luck with that.

>   (KUJI exits. The others wearily file
>   out behind her. NIA stays and puts
>   her hand on IMANI's shoulder. They
>   hug. No words needed. As they clean
>   up the Christmas party clutter...)

IMANI

What is this?
>   (From a pile of holiday junk, IMANI
>   picks up a box.)
A gift. For you, beloved.

NIA

For me?
>   (reading)
Dearest Nia, I might've turnt up a little too much at the Christmas
joint. Blame it on the egg nog. If you're reading this, I'm still
recuperating from a major holiday hangover. You know I hate to miss
a party, especially one in my honor. Give my love to the group.
I'll be there in spirit. Best, Umoja.

>   (NIA hands the card to IMANI and
>   takes the box. NIA opens it,
>   revealing a full kinara set.)

IMANI
>   (reading back of card)
P.S. The grant is for Ujamaa.

NIA
>   (NIA pulls out a fifty dollar bill
>   and pockets it.)
For our troubles.

>   (NIA and IMANI set up the kinara.
>   Then they light the first candle
>   together as CONGA DRUMS rumble from
>   somewhere.)

                    (BLACKOUT)

                    (END OF PLAY)

DRY AND READY

_____

A Play in One Act

by

Matthew J. Kaplan

Cast of Characters

Norma: Female, 60-70s, a former surgeon.
                          Whip-smart. A Jewish Manhattanite,
                          traditionally observant but not
                          extremely religious. Confident and
                          strong, but behind her tough exterior is
                          loneliness, sadness, and regret.

Sam: Gruff, defensive male, 30s-60s.
                          Sam is really just a sweet mama's child.
                          The "leader" and more dominant of the
                          two bumbling thieves. Sam pushes Charlie
                          around, but Sam cares about Charlie, who
                          is his closest thing to a true friend.

Charlie: Male, 30s-60s, sweet, easier going
                          than partner-in-crime, Sam. Despite
                          terrible loneliness, Charlie manages to
                          see the bright side of things, always
                          ready with a smile and an ear to listen.
                          Charlie knows that Sam is more bark
                          than bite and enjoys the friendship and
                          company.

SCENE
Modest, one-bedroom New York City apartment.

TIME
The eighth night of Hanukkah, Present year.

SETTING: A NYC apartment. The living room connects
                                to the kitchen and is illuminated by a
                                menorah's candlelight.

AT RISE: SAM and CHARLIE work on "cracking" a safe.
                                SAM wears a stethoscope to assist with
                                the process.

                    CHARLIE
I'm not sure a stethoscope helps if the safe's combination is
digital. According to the movies I've seen—

                    SAM
Movies? I know what I'm doing. You think this is my first time
cracking a safe?

                    CHARLIE
Yes...

                    SAM
If you don't quiet down, I'm gonna crack your safe.

                    CHARLIE
Sam! Maybe just try 1-2-3-4-5. Most people just use the simplest,
easiest-to-remember passwords and codes.

                    SAM
Oh, you're also an expert on human psychology?

                    CHARLIE
Ya know, Sam, I'm getting tired of the sass!

                    SAM
Shhhhh! You're gonna wake the lady!

                    CHARLIE
Too late.

                    (NORMA, half asleep, walks from her
                    bedroom to the kitchen. They squeeze
                    into a shadowy area. They hold their
                    breath as she drinks some water. She
                    heads back to bed.)

                    SAM
Ok, forget this. Let's just carry the safe outta here.

                        CHARLIE
What? This thing is like 200 pounds!

                          SAM
You have a better idea?

                        CHARLIE
Maybe we can just steal something else?

                          SAM
Like what? Yesterday's *New York Times* and a tub of hummus? We're
here for the safe, so we'll take the safe. Come on, here we go...
aaaand lift!

            (They have great difficulty lifting
            and moving it. They bump into a table
            and knock over the menorah! CHARLIE
            drops the safe. SAM screams. CHARLIE
            jumps on the candles to extinguish
            them. NORMA busts out of her room
            brandishing a scalpel, and turns on
            the lights. All scream.)

                         NORMA
Who the hell are you? What are you doing with my safe?

                          SAM
                     (to CHARLIE)
Nothing, lady. Go back to bed. Come on, let's get this thing outta
here.

                         NORMA
                  (grabbing her phone)
No, you don't! I'm calling the cops...Shit!

                        CHARLIE
What?

                         NORMA
The phone's dead!

                          SAM
                  (struggling to lift)
Perfect! Come on, grab your end!

                         NORMA
                    (finding a charger)
As soon as this phone charges, I'm calling the police. And I'm
gonna take your picture. Don't try to stop me. I know how to use
this scalpel.
                    (Putting on her glasses, she inches
                    towards them.)
Wait a minute. I know you two imbeciles.

                          SAM

I doubt it—

                         NORMA

You're the two shmoes who delivered my bedroom accent chair earlier
today. And now you steal my safe? You were here to—what is it—
case the joint? You cased my joint!

                          SAM

You probably have us mistaken for two other—

                         NORMA

Impossible! I made you lunch! I cooked you latkes—from scratch!
Latkes!

                        CHARLIE

They were delicious, thank you.

                          SAM

Charlie!

                         NORMA
                    (inspecting their faces)
That's right—Charlie! Charlie and Sam. Talk about biting the hand
that feeds you! The shame on you two! Breaking into my house,
scaring me to death, and stealing from me after feeding you and—
                    (she screams)
My rug! The menorah!

                          SAM

It's nothing. We extinguished it before any real damage happened.

                         NORMA

The rug is one thing, but the menorah? Oh, no. Now you guys have
really done it.

                    CHARLIE
Done what?

                    NORMA
You can't extinguish a menorah. And on the eighth night? Oh boy,
this is not good.

                    SAM
Ok, here we go, Charlie. Focus! On three. One, two, three!

            (They grunt and struggle.)

                    NORMA
                (attending to the mess)
Look at all these wasted candles.

                    CHARLIE
Can't you just put new candles in there and relight it?

                    NORMA
No, there are no more candles left. The box contains exactly forty-
four candles. That's enough for eight days, plus the Shamash for
each night.

                    CHARLIE
That's clever. What's the Shamaaa—

                    NORMA
The Shamash. The helper candle. You use it to light the other
candles. It doesn't actually represent its own night of Hanukkah,
it's just there so the other candles can shine bright. Hanukkah
can't happen without it but yet there she sits alone, overworked,
insignificant...

                    CHARLIE
That's so sad.

                    SAM
Oh, please. No one asked for a Hanukkah sob story. Come on—

                    NORMA
My grandmother used to talk about a man in a neighboring village—
Zev Adelman. One night he had too much heavy malaga, knocked over
a menorah, and set off a curse that wiped out all of the village's
livestock.

CHARLIE

A curse?

NORMA

If you extinguish a menorah before it naturally burns out, a
horrible curse is unleashed.

SAM

Ooooh, so scary.
            (to CHARLIE)
Don't listen to any of that mumbo jumbo. Keep moving.

CHARLIE

Sam, can we take a break? It's so heavy. I feel like it's gonna
slip from my hands.

SAM

Focus, Charlie! We're almost outta here.

CHARLIE

Ok, I'm trying...but, ma'am, please, it was an accident, we didn't
mean it.

NORMA

It doesn't matter. A curse is a curse.

SAM

Oh please, enough! Curses aren't real!

NORMA

They're real!

SAM

They're not!

CHARLIE

I'm slipping!

NORMA

They're as real as Santa!

SAM

Don't shit-talk Santa!

                              CHARLIE
      I'm losing my grip!

                              NORMA
      Behold the curse!

                              SAM
      Fuck the curse!

                              CHARLIE
      Saaaam!

                  (The safe slips out of CHARLIE's hands
                  and crashes onto SAM's foot with a
                  loud thud. SAM screams in pain.)

                              SAM
      You idiot! I think you broke my toe!

                              CHARLIE
      I'm sorry, Sam, but it's not my fault. It's probably because of—

                              NORMA
      The curse! We light the candles on Hanukkah to commemorate the
      miracle of oil burning for eight nights during the rebuilding of
      the great temple...
                        (noticing their confusion)
      It's all in the Bible...and the internet. I'd tell you to google
      it, but I can't get that damned computer hooked up to the wifi.
      Anyway, the menorah symbolizes a miracle. And the opposite of a
      miracle is a curse!

                              SAM
      There are no such things as curses! It's ridiculous! It's crazy!
      It's...it's...it's—
                        (He sneezes and eyes widen.)
      My tooth. I sneezed out my tooth!

                        CHARLIE and NORMA
                  (in unison)
      The curse!

                              SAM
      You're both crazy! It's not a curse!

                         NORMA
You sneezed a tooth.

                          SAM
It happens. It's a thing!

                        CHARLIE
Tooth-sneezing is not a thing!

                          SAM
Let's go, Charlie, let's move this safe out before the lady's phone
charges.

                         NORMA
Norma. My name is Norma. I tipped you each for the delivery and I
made you latkes and apple sauce. My name is Norma. And is that a
stethoscope? A child's toy stethoscope?
              (to CHARLIE)
Clearly, you're the brains of this pathetic operation—

                        CHARLIE
Thank you.

                         NORMA
Even an actual stethoscope would not help you with cracking the
combination on a digital safe. Haven't you ever watched any movies?

                          SAM
What are you two, Siskel and Ebert? Charlie! Now!

                         NORMA
Be nice to your friend.

                          SAM
Mind your own business, Norma. Charlie, pick up that end of the
safe and let's move.
              (CHARLIE's phone rings.)

                        CHARLIE
It's my neighbor, Mrs. Kroichek. Why would she be calling at this
hour—Hello? Yes...Oh, oh no! What? Is he? And you ...Okay, okay,
I'll be there as soon as I can. Please text with updates. Thank
you, thank you, Mrs. Kroichek.

                         NORMA
Everything okay?

                        CHARLIE
There was a fire in my building. It's minor but there was smoke in
the halls. When Mrs. Kroichek didn't see me downstairs, she alerted
the firemen. They broke down the door and, and, and Maurice—

                         NORMA
Maurice?

                          SAM
Charlie's dog—

                        CHARLIE
He inhaled too much smoke. Mrs. Kroichek is at the vet with him
now...the curse! It's the curse! Norma! What do we have to do to
stop it?

                          SAM
There's no curse! Only safe-stealing! Now pick up your end!

                        CHARLIE
No!

                          SAM
Fine, I'll do it myself!

                    (SAM attempts to pick up the safe.
                    He struggles and screams, freezing
                    in a bent over position.)

                        CHARLIE
See? See!

                          SAM
See what? Come here and help me!

                        CHARLIE
                    (rushing over)
Sam. Please. We are in the middle of a crazy Hanukkah curse. And if
we don't do anything about it...my Maurice!

                          SAM
He is a cute dog.

                           CHARLIE
The cutest.

                            SAM
He's got that little wet nose.

                           CHARLIE
The wettest!

                            SAM
I can't believe I'm doing this. Fine. Norma, what do we do about
this curse? Will doing that help my back?

                           NORMA
No, simply standing up straight will help your back.

                            SAM
                (standing)
Oh, well look at that. What are you, some kind of a doctor?

                           NORMA
Some kind. More on that another time. But for now, we have to worry
about Maurice.

                           CHARLIE
Thank you, Norma. What do we have to do to reverse the curse?

                           NORMA
The first step to redemption is sharing joy with those that you have
done wrong. So let's sing some Hanukkah songs!

                           CHARLIE
Oh fun! I know one.
                (singing)
Oh, dreidel dreidel dreidel...

                     NORMA and CHARLIE
                (in unison)
*I made it out of clay and when it's dry and ready, oh dreidel I
will play...*

                           CHARLIE
Come on, Sam!

                            SAM
No! Enough! Stop with the singing! I don't sing. No one should
sing. If you want us to do something, give us some real work!

                    NORMA
Jeesh. Somebody's got a brick in their babka. Fine, real work...
who's good with computers?

                    CHARLIE
I was fired from the Apple Store.

                    NORMA
Perfect! Okay, so, I can't connect that fakakta computer to the
internet. Go ahead. All of the passwords are written on that giant
piece of oak tag.

              (CHARLIE sits on the couch and opens a
              laptop. He inspects a gigantic piece
              of paper with large writing.)

                    CHARLIE
You really should keep these passwords in a safer place.

                    NORMA
Oh like in a safe? What if a bunch of yutzes break into my home
and steal the safe?

                    SAM
What's a yutz?

                    NORMA
You. And you're the yutz who's gonna wash my dishes.

                    SAM
Dishes?

                    NORMA
Yes. Remember those latkes I made for you and your friend?

                    CHARLIE
They were delicious!

                    NORMA
The pots and pans used to make them. The dishes you ate from?
They're in the sink.

                    SAM
I don't do dishes.

                         NORMA
Would you rather do my laundry?

                          SAM
I'll do the dishes!

                    (SAM goes to the kitchen. NORMA moves
                    to CHARLIE who is stretching a hand
                    and wincing in pain.)

                         NORMA
What's happening with your wrist there, Charlie?

                        CHARLIE
Oh, just some stiffness. I'm okay.

                         NORMA
Let me see.

                    (NORMA takes CHARLIE's arm and feels
                    in the armpit area. CHARLIE jumps and
                    giggles.)

                        CHARLIE
It's my wrist, not my armpit.

                         NORMA
Actually, I think it's your median nerve, which starts in the
armpit and moves down your arm and into your wrist.
                    (massaging CHARLIE's wrist)
It feels swollen, indicating carpal tunnel. You should get this
checked out. But for now, back to work.

                          SAM
Seriously, what's the deal? Are you a doctor or not?

                         NORMA
I was. Oh, I was...

                    (NORMA moves to the window and
                    stares into the night.)

                          SAM
And?

NORMA

And I'm not getting into it now.

CHARLIE

You'll feel better if you get it off your chest. Please?

NORMA

I didn't realize I'd be sharing tonight, but fine, yes, I was a doctor. An orthopedic surgeon. Top of my class, and all that. I was following in my father's footsteps. But in addition to inheriting my father's skills with the scalpel, I also picked up some of his other less respectable habits. He liked to drink. I loved getting high. And a junkie with a prescription pad is a dangerous combination.

CHARLIE

Oh Norma, I'm so sorry. You lost your license?

NORMA

I did.

SAM

You don't look like a junkie.

NORMA

I've been in recovery for thirty-four years. But I'll always be a junkie.

CHARLIE

Did your father also lose his license?

NORMA

Yeah right. He was a man. And he practiced medicine in the fifties. They smoked cigarettes in the operating room! He could have gotten away with murder. Things have changed.

SAM

Can't you get your license back? With good behavior or whatever?

NORMA

Sure, I suppose. But why? I fucked up. I threw it away. What's the point? I had my chance, and I squandered it.

CHARLIE

But Norma—

NORMA

But nothing. I was a good doctor but a lousy person. I don't deserve another chance, and I'm tired of talking about myself. What's your deal? You guys have jobs. You delivered my chair. They must pay you. So tell me, what's with the burglary?

SAM

Hey look, I'm sorry, I'm sorry! I'm washing your dishes and—oh, where can I find a Brillo pad or something?

NORMA

Under the sink.

SAM

Thanks...and we're not stealing your safe anymore. We'll make good on any trouble we caused, and then we'll be on our way.

NORMA

But why? Why do you steal?

SAM

Because maybe delivery drivers don't get paid as much as doctors, or anyone else. We got bills to pay. We have responsibilities, people we need to care for.

NORMA
(moving closer to SAM)

I see. Well, I told you my story. So dishwasher, go ahead and dish. Tell me, who are you taking care of? Kids? A spouse? Spouses?

SAM

No, it's my ma. She'll be 90 in March. We're gonna have a big party. I have a guy coming over to sing Sinatra—

NORMA

That's nice.

SAM

—but most days, she can't really take care of herself anymore. Medicare is lousy. I gotta pay the home health aids outta pocket. My salary doesn't cover that.

NORMA

I'm sorry. That's rough. It's fucked up, and it's not fair. I don't know what to say, Sam, but stealing?

                         SAM
What choice do I have?

                        NORMA
Good question, and I wish I had an answer for you.
                    (to CHARLIE)
And what about you? Who are you taking care of?

                       CHARLIE
Just Maurice.
                (looking at phone)
I hope he's okay. Oh, Maurice...

                        NORMA
Okay, I've had pets. Your salary must cover that. Soooo, please, do
tell, why do you steal?
                       CHARLIE
I, uh...I like it.

                        NORMA
You like it? You broke into my home and nearly gave me a heart
attack! You knocked over my menorah, you burned my rug because you
like it? Are you serious?

                       CHARLIE
I am.

                        NORMA
Okay, fine. I'll play along. What exactly is it that you like about
stealing from others?

                       CHARLIE
The stuff. People's stuff. I like seeing people's stuff. I like
knowing what things are part of their lives. Where they went, what
they like. I like thinking that maybe they gave me these things. I
don't get many gifts or anything. Other than Maurice, I don't really
have anyone that's close to me and I just...I know it's silly, but
I feel like having other people's things makes me closer to them.

                        NORMA
Oh, boy. I don't know whether to call Bellevue or give you a giant
hug.

                       CHARLIE
I like hugs.

                    NORMA
Finish with my computer, and then we'll negotiate further
exchanges.

                    CHARLIE
Oh, I finished that already. You're all connected. Now I'm just
googling, looking for info about this curse. I don't actually see
anything.

                    NORMA
You're not looking in the right place.

                    CHARLIE
Is there even a curse at all?

                    SAM
Dishes are done!

                    CHARLIE
Did you just make that up? You've kept us here.

                    NORMA
You chose to be here.

                    SAM
I did dishes for nothing?

                    CHARLIE
My dog. Maurice. He's suffering at the vet, I don't know if he'll
be okay. I need to see him.

                    SAM
I have dish-pan hands!

                    CHARLIE
You lied to us! There's no curse! You did this just to keep us here
because you're just as sad and lonely as the rest of us. There's
never been a curse, we did all this stuff, nothing's different,
it's just all your bull—
              (He gets a text. He laughs.)
He's okay! Maurice is okay! Mrs. Kroichek, sent a picture!

                    NORMA
Oh, look at that fuzzy face.

                        CHARLIE
Oh god, I'm so sorry, Norma. I was just upset.

                        NORMA
It's okay. Is there a curse? I don't know. Maybe. I've heard that.
My people have a lot of ways of interpreting things. Even the
holiday itself, Hanukkah, can be spelled a few different ways. Our
traditions are designed to keep scholars debating. So, who knows,
maybe there's a curse, maybe there isn't. Either way, you are both
forgiven.

                        SAM
Thank you. But what about you?

                        NORMA
Me?

                        SAM
Have you forgiven yourself?

                        NORMA
For what? Eating cereal for dinner? Watching too much TV?

                        SAM
No. For, ya know, what happened with your career. Addiction is a
disease. You're in recovery. You can't spend the rest of your life
blaming yourself for what happened years ago.

                        NORMA
Oh, wow. Look who's Captain Sensitivity all of the sudden.

                        SAM
I know I can be gruff. I'm sorry. And I'm sorry to you too,
Charlie.

                        CHARLIE
Thanks, buddy.

                        SAM
Look, Norma. It's Hanukkah. You exchange gifts on Hanukkah, right?
So give yourself the gift of forgiveness.

                        NORMA
Oh, that's clever...shit, you're right. You are, I know you are,
but I don't even know how to forgive myself at this point. It's

NORMA (cont.)

easier to hold onto the pain and just lock it away. Oh! Speaking of, I have some gifts for you. Charlie, open that safe. The combination is 1-2-3-4-5.

CHARLIE
(to SAM)

See?

(CHARLIE opens the safe and removes a stethoscope.)

NORMA

That's for Sam. You should throw away that toy one, but only if you promise me that you won't use it for stealing.

SAM

I'm not sure I can make that promise. How else can I afford to take care of my mom?

CHARLIE

I know, I know! Norma, you can take care of her! Forgive yourself by doing what you love, by doing what you do best.

SAM

But I can't afford that—

NORMA

You don't have to. Charlie, you're right. Sam, I'm going to start helping with your mom. No charge. Where do you live?

SAM

I'm in Brooklyn, right off Flatbush Avenue.

NORMA

Brooklyn? Really? Are you at least near Junior's?

SAM

Right around the corner.

NORMA

Fine. I require one slice of cheesecake on Fridays.

SAM

You have a deal!

                    NORMA
And Charlie, I was going to give you the rest of that medical
equipment but I guess I'll need it now.

                    CHARLIE
That's okay. I really don't need anything. That is, unless you were
making more latkes.

                    NORMA
They're way too greasy to have more than once per year, but I was
planning on making some chicken meatballs this weekend, so if—

                    CHARLIE
Can I bring Maurice?

                    NORMA
Of course.

                    CHARLIE
Thank you, and Norma, my Hanukkah gift to you is to share joy. Lots
of it! So my friends, let us sing!
                    (singing)
Ohhhh...Dreidel, dreidel, dreidel...

                    (NORMA joins CHARLIE. SAM reluctantly
                    sings too. They sing themselves out the
                    front door. NORMA continues humming,
                    turns off the light and heads into
                    her bedroom.)

                    (BLACKOUT)

                    (END OF PLAY)

ALL MIRACLES ARE GREAT MIRACLES

A Play in One Act

by

Yangzhou (Yao) Bian

Cast of Characters

Bubbe:
Male, 70s. The rabbi emeritus of the synagogue. Father to Shimon and Sholom. Grandfather to Lilian and Liliah. A charismatic Jew, with a biting tongue and a daunting perspective.

Sholom:
Male, 40s-50s. The chef. The twin to Shimon.

Shimon:
Male, 40s-50s. The rabbi. The twin to Sholom. Father to Lilian and Liliah.

Lilian:
Female, five to eight years old. The elder of the sisters. Playful.

Liliah:
Female, five to eight years old. Youngest sister. Mischievous.

Boy:
Male, 13-15, dumb. Lives at the shelter, but no one knows where he's from.

Woman's Voice:
Sholom and Shimon's mother who feverishly works in the kitchen offstage.

SCENE
The family home

TIME
Hanukkah

SETTING: Chairs and a dinner table with a
                            tablecloth and tableware. In the center
                            stands a menorah. To stage right is the
                            exit, and upstage is the entrance to the
                            kitchen.

AT RISE: Empty seats around the dinner table.

                    WOMAN'S VOICE (O.S.)
What's this, Sholom? What do you want me to do? Turn air into a
dish? Get on your toes! We have fourteen stomachs to fill!

                       SHOLOM (O.S.)
Yes, yes! What shall I get? Salt? Sugar? Milk? Flour? Or would you
like a glass of water?

                    WOMAN'S VOICE (O.S.)
Get your senses!
                (BUBBE enters from stage right,
                followed by BOY holding a covered
                cage in his hand.)
Sholom, what are you standing here for? Go and get the apples!
Don't tell me you are waiting for them to fall from the branches
and roll into the pans! I am not going to be the one to announce to
the family that we forgot the sauce again!

                        SHOLOM
                (runs on stage)
Yes! Apples! Apples! Apples!

                (SHOLOM runs into BOY. He searches
                around BOY as if BOY is an apple
                tree. He looks in front, then behind,
                SHOLOM lifts BOY's arm, looks up and
                under, and puts BOY's arms down.
                SHOLOM pats around BOY's clothes to
                see if there are apples somewhere.
                SHOLOM scratches his head and turns
                around.)

                        BUBBE
Shimon.
                (sound of wind as all shiver)
Shut the door.

                            SHOLOM
Yes, the door—
                    (shuts the door and reaches out his
                  arms to BUBBE)
Father, what are you doing out there in all this chill? And who is
the—

                            BUBBE
                  (takes the bird cage from BOY, and
                    puts it in SHOLOM's hand)
Couldn't you see? Tevye got out again.

                            SHOLOM
Oh no, not again, the poor friend. I am glad you brought her back.
She never figured out the way home, not for once.

                            BUBBE
And we never figured out why she was going.

                            SHOLOM
Father, you could have called me or Shimon! But you, yourself
alone, and in such weather!

                            BUBBE
What are you yelling about, Shimon? You are not as blind, and I am
not as deaf.

                            SHOLOM
Father, I am Sholom. With all that ice—

                            BUBBE
                  (removes scarf and wraps it around
                  SHOLOM's neck)
That's what I am saying, Shimon. With that storm going on...
                    (removes jacket and hangs it on
                  SHOLOM's elbow)
...hadn't it been for the young man, I'd have no way to get Tevye
home without getting my legs broken or hips fractured. Then you
and your brother would have to pay, and pay for the emergency room
visit. Hadn't it been for the boy, we'd all be spending Hanukkah
there, and spending the money we ought to be spending on Hanukkah
on Medicare.

                            SHOLOM
Father, would you like to have something—

                         BUBBE
                  (taking the bird cage)
I am delivering the owl to the lady.

                        SHOLOM
                      (lectures)
Father, Mother could wait. Rest yourself and take something warm.
It's no kidding catching a cold. Instead of slurping the matzo ball
soup, you'd be blowing your nose over the dinner table. Instead of
an appetite, you'd be stressing over a headache. Last year, it was
absolutely miserable watching you watch us finish the sufganiyot
from the first to last. And this year, we are adding new flavors to
donuts!

                         BUBBE
Shimon, I admire your enthusiasm for food—

                        SHOLOM
                    (enthusiastic)
Father, food is unmistakably art! Had you seen the desserts, you'd
not be able to remove yourself from the tray without reaching for a
bite—

                         BUBBE
Shimon, save the speech for the table. My boy, there is to be no
delay, or both your mother and Tevye will be due for a fit. And that
would have the dinner ruined before it even gets started.

                        SHOLOM
Father, no Jew loses their temper on Hanukkah!

                  (The sound of falling, cracking, and
                  chaos.)

                  WOMAN'S VOICE (O.S.)
Who the heck put eggs here? I swear I am gonna—oh, God watch over
the brisket!

                  (The sound of rushing footsteps.)

                         BUBBE
Shimon, sometimes we are made to face what we are despite—

                        SHOLOM
                    (rushing off)
One second!

                         BUBBE
...who we are.
                  (to BOY)
My friend, make yourself at home. Have him get you whatever you
need.
                  (BOY shakes his head.)
I forgot you don't speak. In that case, take all that he has to
offer. Others, you could not be quite sure, but Shimon? He has no
taste for bad stuff. Shimon. Where is Shimon?

                         SHOLOM
                  (rushes on stage and stops in front
                  of BUBBE and BOY)
Here he is.
                  (offers his hand to BOY)
I am Sholom.
                  (reckons the panpipe hanging around BOY's neck)
You are a musician?

                  (BOY hides behind BUBBE.)

                         BUBBE
Shimon—

                         SHOLOM
Sholom.

                         BUBBE
Shimon—

                         SHOLOM
Sholom.

                         BUBBE
Shylock.

                         SHOLOM
                  (jumps)
Shylock! No! Father, we are not playing Merchant of Venice.

                         BUBBE
Just checking. Shimon—

                         SHOLOM
Sholom.

BUBBE

That's what it is!
> (to BOY)

When you've got a twin of two and a wife that insists on the twin of two names.
> (to SHOLOM)

Shimon, I leave you with this. It is good that you understand this is no Shakespearean drama. While we are all for merriment, rededication is not the time to play a stereotype that is unrelated to our traditions. Remember, no Shylock.

SHOLOM

No.

BUBBE

No, no. Shylock.

SHOLOM

Father, you've my word in front of the menorah.

BUBBE
> (grabs menorah)

The menorah. It is made of gold, isn't it?

SHOLOM

I believe so. Shimon's father-in-law was a man of fortune. The menorah was a wedding gift to the groom and the bride.

BUBBE
> (hands it to BOY)

Take it to the shelter.
> (BOY shakes his head.)

You people will need it more than us for the coming year. It is going to get harder. The President is exhausting the funds on the border. There are not going to be resources for public welfare.

SHOLOM

Father, you may want to speak to Shimon.

BUBBE

Shimon, Your brother Sholom has a better notion of himself than he purports to be.

                              SHOLOM
                  (putting the menorah in BOY's bag)
We will pack some food along with it before the serving of dinner.
                         (to BOY)
I wish there are more that we could share.

                              BUBBE
Shimon, the prayer is always to ask for more to spare. But the
mitzvah is to share what you have, not what you will get.

                    (BUBBE exits. LILIAN and LILIAH run
                    to the table with Hanukkah gelt in
                    their arms and a wooden dreidel. The
                    girls make a playstation out of the
                    corner of the table.)

                              LILIAN
Shin, shin, shin, put your pieces in!

                              LILIAH
Gimmel, gimmel, gimmel, I shall have it all!

                              LILIAN
                    (draws the Hanukkah gelt towards
                    her)
You lost! These are mine!

                              LILIAH
                    (draws the Hanukkah gelt back)
You lied! These are mine!

                              LILIAN
That's a shin!

                              LILIAH
That's a gimmel!

                    (BOY looks at the girls.)

                              SHOLOM
The girls are playing dreidel. Would you like to join?
                    (BOY nods, then shakes his head.)
No worries, let us get you seated.

                    (SHOLOM leads BOY to the empty chair
                    next to LILIAN and LILIAH.)

            (He takes the Hanukkah gelt from the
            girls, and puts them in front of BOY.)

                        LILIAN and LILIAH
Uncle!

                            SHOLOM
                (to BOY)
Have a try. These are handmade chocolates, the real ones. Not
the factory produced ones from the candy section at the markets.
Indulge the tongue, or let the kids win them back.

                (BOY picks up a piece of Hanukkah
                gelt, confused.)

                            SHOLOM
You don't know this, do you?
                (takes dreidel)
Yes, let me—

                        WOMAN'S VOICE (O.S.)
Sholom! The latkes are all turning black! Are you getting us fed,
or are you getting our food burned?

                            SHOLOM
I am coming! Coming!
                (to the kids)
Lilian, and Liliah, show him the game.
                (to BOY)
I will check back. If you want anything, just yell—

                        WOMAN'S VOICE (O.S.)
Sholom!

                            SHOLOM
                (to BOY)
Like that.

                        WOMAN'S VOICE (O.S.)
Where are the onions? What are these shallots hanging about here?

                            SHOLOM
The scallions are in the sink—
                (to LILIAN and LILIAH)
Be friendly and polite—

                    WOMAN'S VOICE (O.S.)
Scallions! We are not doing Christmas Eve Asian take-out! Not when
I am wearing the apron. Sholom! Where are you dawdling about? And
where are the apples?

                    SHOLOM
          (rushes offstage)
On my heels! On my heels!

                    LILIAN
          (to BOY)
I'm Lilian.

                    LILIAH
          (to BOY)
I'm Liliah.

          (BOY stares blankly.)

                    LILIAN
Is he mute?

                    LILIAH
Are you mute?

                    LILIAN
He's got all our coins.

                    LILIAH
And he is not a Jew.

                    LILIAN
Liliah, I have got a—
               (She whispers. LILIAH nods.)
Uncle said you are playing dreidel with us.

                    LILIAH
You want to.

                    LILIAN
We will show you the rules.

                    LILIAH
And the tricks. Oh, no, not the tricks.

                    LILIAN
The top has four sides.

                    LILIAH
On each, there is a letter.

                    LILIAN
          (spins the dreidel)
It is the non, which means you could not touch my coins.

          (She takes the Hannukah gelt that
          SHOLOM took from her.)

                    LILIAH
Now, I am playing.
          (spins the dreidel)
It is the gimmel, which means you should give me half of your
coins.
          (Takes half of the remaining gelt
          from BOY's pile and gives him the
          dreidel.)
It is your turn.

          (BOY spins.)

                    LILIAN
He is got hei!

                    LILIAH
Hei is host, which is—you are to hand out the whole of your
possessions.

          (They each take half of BOY's
          remaining coins.)

                    LILIAN
Now, next—
          (spins)
Oh no, shin! This means...this means, you shall shake out a few
more coins for the sake of others.

                    LILIAH
But Lilian, he's broke.

                    LILIAN
When you run out of coins, you can always borrow.

                         LILIAH
                (puts two in BOY's pot)
If we lend you two, you'd pay double.

                         LILIAN
                (puts three in BOY's pot)
If we lend you three, you will hand us back triple, or you could
trade the panpipe with us.

                    (BOY covers the panpipe with both
                    hands.)

                         LILIAH
Okay, okay, she is just saying. Take your gelt.

                    (BOY takes a gelt and starts to
                    peel.)

                         LILIAN
                    (takes the coin and puts it back in
                    her pile)
No, no, no, you cannot eat the gelt when you are in debt.

                    LILIAN and LILIAH
Get it? Let's roll!

                    (BOY stands and walks towards the
                    audience while the girls play. Light
                    shifts.)

                         BOY
                (gestures to back wall projection
                with a prerecorded voice)
I used to have a voice. Since very little, I was with the "Rat
Grandmama". She picked Snow and me up on the road. We traveled
around the countries, driving the ones that nag and gnaw out of the
homes. Three years ago, this town was plagued by rodents—rodents
the size of cats and dogs. So we came here. "Rat Grandmama" would
blow the pipe, and I would chant while Snow hooted. The pests would
run and run until they reached the rivers and the lakes and drowned
themselves. The area was almost cleaned. Here, was the site of
the last battle. It was the toughest night I ever lived. Snow was
severely injured, fending the children from the teeth and claws. I
fainted from exhaustion. When I woke up, I was at the shelter, and
"Rat Grandmama" was sitting by my side. After that day, I could not
make a sound.

BOY (cont.)
(reveals scar on his throat)
"Rat Grandmama" said a hex was buried in the scratch. Because of this, we could not work anymore. We stayed so that we could see Snow. The family took her in and slowly, they nursed her back. Last week, "Rat Grandmama" passed away. She died of rabies, left to her from a bite from the Queen of the Mice.
(takes out the pipe and blows)
Snow was trying to get out to see her, but she couldn't make it until this morning. The three of us sang our last song together. In silence.
(prays)
Snow left, and the shelter was closing. I packed my belongings and thought I would be on the way. Snow flew back with such urgency and dragged me to the old gentleman who was lying on the bottom of a slope, holding a birdcage to his chest. We brought him to the shelter. The Doctor examined him and fixed up the few scratches. The old gentleman insisted on returning home.

BUBBE
(offstage)
It is a very important holiday.

BOY
So the Doctor sent me back with him, and he invited me in.

BUBBE
(appears in the spotlight on the
other side of the stage)
Generosity carries on with generosity.

BOY
(prerecorded voice)
Kindness continues with kindness.

BUBBE
And the story.

(BUBBE disappears. Light changes as
BOY returns to his seat.)

SHIMON
(enters with a box of candles)
Lilian, Liliah! See what I have got?

                    LILIAN and LILIAH
                (running towards SHIMON)
Colored candles!

                    SHIMON
Outside it is getting dark. It's time to light the menorah.

                    LILIAN
Let me light the first candle!

                    LILIAH
Daddy, I want to light the first one!

                    LILIAN
Daddy, me!

                    LILIAH
Daddy, please!

                    SHIMON
One at a time, one at a time.

                    LILIAN
                (reaches for the candle box)
Let me do it! Liliah did it last year!

                    LILIAH
                (reaches for the candle box)
Let me do it! Lilian almost set the curtain on fire the year before
last!
                    LILIAN
                (tugs LILIAH)
You cannot do it again!

                    LILIAH
                (tugs back)
You cannot do it right!

                    LILIAN
Let go! Or I'll fight!

                    LILIAH
Leave me, or I'll bite!

                         SHIMON
If so...

                    LILIAN and LILIAH
If so?

                         SHIMON
I am doing it. Bring the matchbox.

                    LILIAN and LILIAH
This is not fair!

                         SHIMON
Where is the menorah? It was sitting on the table the whole
afternoon!

                         LILIAN
             (climbs up the table)
Not here!

                         LILIAH
             (sniffs under the table)
Nothing here!

                         SHIMON
The gold Chanukiah...
                  (Picks BOY up from his seat to look
                  around.)
Your mother would have skinned me alive...
                  (Puts BOY down to the side.)
Lilian, you've gained quite a bit of weight—
                  (BOY taps SHIMON on the shoulder,
                  and SHIMON points the candle box at
                  BOY.)
Who are you?
                  (BOY raises his hands.)
Talk!

                         LILIAN
Daddy, the thief!

                         LILIAH
Is he the thief?

                         LILIAN
Someone must be.

                        LILIAH
How do we know?

                        LILIAN
I don't. Do you?

                        LILIAH
He is not one of us...is he?

                    SHIMON
            (points the candle box at BOY)
Who—are—you?

            (BOY removes menorah from his bag.)

                    LILIAN and LILIAH
He is the thief!

                    SHIMON
            (aims the candle box at BOY)
Surrender the Chanukiah!

            (BOY hands the menorah over, SHIMON
            snatches the menorah and BUBBE
            snatches the menorah from SHIMON.)

                    SHOLOM
            (runs out, aiming ladle at SHIMON)
Let go of the candle box!

                    SHIMON
            (aims the candle box around, then at
            BUBBE)
Let go of the menorah!
            (BUBBE hits SHIMON with the menorah,
            and he ducks)
Father! You could not hit a man with a menorah!

                    BUBBE
Bullying a guest! Sholom, God would have struck you down with the
Torah!

                    SHIMON
Father, I am Shimon...

BUBBE
I know you are Sholom, your brother is never as dumb.

SHIMON
Father! You've seen with your own eyes! We've got a thief! No clue
who is the dunce that let him in...
                (waves around candle box)
If I am to find out—

BUBBE
I am that dunce, and I gave the candelabrum to the boy to take to
the shelter. Are you going to beat me up with candlesticks?

SHIMON
To the shelter? Father, are you mad? Those lazybones, they've none
of working but knocking on people's doors begging for charity!

BUBBE
Sholom, if you could do charity then you would not have to do work.
Have you had that time to blame others, you might use it to reflect
on your conduct.
                (hands the menorah to BOY)
Come here, my friend. Please accept the menorah along with my
apologies.

SHIMON
                (stands in the way)
Father, I implore you to think! The Chanukiah is a divine object!
You cannot have a stranger to—

SHOLOM
Shimon, we were all once strangers.

SHIMON
He is a stranger to our faith!

SHOLOM
To God, no one is a stranger. Shimon, the son of God is bound by
faith as much as by the generosity of the spirit and the kindness
of heart.

SHIMON
Generosity! He is after our money!

SHOLOM
He has found Tevye.

SHIMON

A Snow Owl!

BUBBE

Do you have an issue with a Snow Owl?

LILIAN
(vehemently)
Daddy, Daddy! Tevye is not just a Snow Owl!

SHIMON

An owl is an owl!

LILIAN

Tevye is our owl! She protected us-

LILIAH and LILIAN
(at SHIMON)
She preserved us from those giant rats!

LILIAN

She held them by the tail and threw them out of the window!

LILIAH

Then there were hundreds of them jumping at us all at once!

LILIAN

She spread her wings over us!

LILIAH

They dug their nails into her flesh, but she didn't move!

LILIAN

They plucked out her plumage, and she didn't budge!

LILIAH
(fearful)
If it wasn't for Teyve, I would have lost my eyes...

LILIAN
(fearful)
If it wasn't for Teyve, I would not have kept my nose...

SHIMON

Fine, fine, Tevye is a special owl. But what has that to do with the menorah?

BUBBE

The boy is to have the menorah.

SHIMON

Father, you are insane! He'd melt it for the gold and this would be the last you'd see of the candelabrum!

BUBBE

Why not? In his hands, it keeps the home for the homeless. In your keeping, it sits in the cabinet accumulating dust aside from seven days out of a year.

SHIMON

It's my wife's candelabrum!

BUBBE

It's God's menorah.

SHIMON

I am not giving permission!

SHOLOM

Shimon, the light of God is the light of sharing.

BUBBE
            (to SHOLOM)
Shimon, had you been less occupied with the kitchen, you'd have made a better example for the congregation.

SHOLOM
            (shirks from BUBBE and holds up the
            ladle)
I serve God through cooking!

SHIMON
            (snatching the menorah)
Father, a beggar is a beggar. If that one is truly deserving, God would have performed a miracle.

BUBBE

It will take a miracle to make you a deserving rabbi.

                    SHIMON
I am the Jews' rabbi!

                    BUBBE
You ought to be God's and the people's rabbi.

                    SHIMON
I am not going to let—

            (BOY takes out the panpipe and blows
            "Ma'oz Tzur". The stage goes black.
            Flames rise one after another.)

                    LILIAN
It is lit without candles!

                    LILIAH
It is flaming without fire!

            (BOY hands the menorah to SHIMON. A
            moment. SHIMON blesses BOY. SHIMON
            hands the menorah back to him. The
            family hums the "Rock of Ages". BOY
            touches his throat. Slowly BOY opens
            his mouth and starts to sing. LILIAN
            and LILIAH pass the Hanukkah gelt to
            the others and the audience.)

                    BUBBE
Chag sameach, and may you have a blissful Hanukkah.

                    (BLACKOUT)

                    (END OF PLAY)

ANGELS UNAWARES

_____

A Play in One Act

by

Melanie Payne

Cast of Characters

<u>José</u>:	Young hispanic man, 20-25.
<u>María</u>:	Young hispanic woman, 16-20.
<u>Sister Melchora</u>:	A woman over 40.
<u>Sister Baltazar</u>:	A woman over 40.
<u>Sister Gaspar</u>:	A woman over 40.
<u>La Dueña</u>:	A woman over 40.

<u>SCENE</u>
Self-storage facility

<u>TIME</u>
Christmas Eve and Christmas Day, Present day

<u>ACT I</u>

<u>SCENE 1</u>

SETTING: Next door is a self-storage facility.
                           Across the road is a large car dealership
                           with a big Christmas tree atop a cell
                           phone tower.

AT RISE: JOSÉ and MARÍA arrive in front of a small
                           hotel on a moped.

                          JOSÉ
We have to stop. Here's a hotel. We'll get a room. It's the only
one I've seen that doesn't have a "No Vacancy" light.

                          MARÍA
I'm so uncomfortable. I need to lie down. I ache all over my body.

                          JOSÉ
Let me handle it Maria.
                    (JOSÉ goes to the front desk. A
                    woman is behind the counter.)
Señora, we would like a room.

                          LA DUEÑA
I don't have any rooms. I'm sorry. We're full. It's Southwest
Florida. It's season, and with the cold up north, people are coming
down before Christmas for the first time since I remember.

                          JOSÉ
                    (dropping his head)
You were the only hotel that didn't have a "No Vacancy" sign. You
were our last hope.

                          LA DUEÑA
Oh, son. That sign hasn't worked in 2,000 years.

                          JOSÉ
I don't know what to do. My wife is pregnant and...

                          LA DUEÑA
Look, I manage the storage unit facility next door. I've got a
unit filled with furniture and the people haven't paid. There's a
mattress in there. It will hold you for a night.

                              JOSÉ
I don't know.

                            LA DUEÑA
I can even give you some sheets and blankets and you can make up
the bed. Seriously, you don't want to be sleeping in the car on
Christmas Eve. And with a pregnant wife, it will be a whole lot
better than riding around on that scooter you got out there. And as
you know, you're not going to find a place.

                              JOSÉ
I guess you're right. Thanks. We'll take it.

                            LA DUEÑA
I'll show you the way.
                    (LA DUEÑA gathers some towels, pillows,
                    linens and blankets, puts them in a
                    laundry basket, and leads JOSÉ and
                    MARÍA to the storage unit. She opens
                    the overhead door and reveals a twin
                    mattress on the floor, boxes stacked
                    against the wall.)
Here you go kids. It's a nice night. The breeze will keep the
mosquitoes away. And you can keep this door cracked so you can get
light and air. There's a comet going by tonight. You should get a
good view of it from here. And that big Christmas tree on top of
the car dealership over there should give you enough light.

                              JOSÉ
Gracias señora. I don't know how to thank you.

                    (MARÍA groans.)

                            LA DUEÑA
Are you alright sweetie pie? That baby is sitting mighty low. Are
you sure you shouldn't be going to the hospital?

                             MARÍA
No, señora, gracias. The baby is not due for another month. I'm
fine. It's from sitting on the bike so long.

                            LA DUEÑA
Well then, I'll say good night to you two. My husband is due back
tomorrow. He's a long distance trucker and should pull in around
five tomorrow afternoon. Please be gone by then, okay?

                         JOSÉ
No problem. And again, thank you.

                 (LA DUEÑA exits.)

                         MARÍA
José, I need to lay down. And you need to help me.

                         JOSÉ
María, let's please go to the hospital.

                         MARÍA
I can't. You know that. They will take the baby away, and they will
deport me. I tried to get to Our Mother's Home but they didn't have
room. It was my last chance.
                 (MARÍA chokes back a scream. JOSÉ
                 puts her on the mattress. She kneels
                 and begins to cry and pant.)
My water broke when we were at the gas station earlier. It's coming,
José. The baby is coming. I can feel it.

                         JOSÉ
Yes, I see María. Push. Push.
                 (JOSÉ picks up the baby from between
                 MARÍA's legs. It starts to cry. He
                 puts the baby on her chest. He takes
                 a pocket knife from his jeans and cuts
                 the cord. Then he goes to the laundry
                 basket and pulls out some towels,
                 wipes off the baby, and wraps him up.
                 MARÍA and the baby fall asleep. He
                 pulls out his phone.)
It's after midnight. It's Christmas, María. Merry Christmas.
                 (He takes the sleeping baby softly
                 away and puts him in the laundry basket
                 next to the mattress. JOSÉ lays down
                 and snuggles against MARÍA.)
I do not care who fathered this baby. I will love him with all of
my heart. He is a gift.

                 (BLACKOUT)

                 (END OF SCENE)

<u>ACT I</u>

<u>SCENE 2</u>

SETTING: The sun is beginning to rise and we hear a
                   car engine in front of the storage unit.

AT RISE: JOSÉ and MARIA awaken to three women
                   ducking under the door of the storage
                   unit. Startled, Maria grabs her baby.

                         MARÍA
Migra! Migra!

                         SISTER MELCORA
Quiet girl. That little baby is sleeping away and you'll wake him
up.

                         JOSÉ
Who are you?

                         SISTER BALTAZAR
Well, we aren't immigration that's for sure, and we're not the law.

                         JOSÉ
Where are you from?

                         SISTER GASPAR
Immokalee.

                         JOSÉ
Immokalee?

                         SISTER GASPAR
East of here.

                         MARÍA
What are you doing here?

                         SISTER GASPAR
We brought you some supplies and things for the baby. Sister
Melocra is a midwife...we're a little late for the birth but she
will want to check you out.

                         SISTER MELCORA
Didn't you call Our Mother's Home?

                        MARÍA
Yes, but the woman who answered said it was full.

                    SISTER BALTAZAR
Well, it was full, but we were sending an intervention team. That's
us. We would have found a place for you until we could get you in.
The volunteer thought you didn't understand, so we tried to call
you back, but you didn't answer.

                        JOSÉ
It said private number. I didn't want to pick up.

                    SISTER BALTAZAR
Oh, yes. We do that for security reasons.

                        MARÍA
How did you find us?

                    SISTER MELCORA
That would be Sister Baltazar. She's a computer whiz. You called
from a cell phone, and she tracked the signal. We lost you for a
while, and then your boyfriend there must have turned it on, and we
picked you right up. We rushed here as fast as we could.

                        MARÍA
I don't want to be deported.

                    SISTER BALTAZAR
Well, that's where Sister Gaspar comes in. She's an immigration
lawyer. She's going to help you. You just have to explain the
situation to her.

                        JOSÉ
It's a little complicated.

                    SISTER BALTAZAR
We've got nothing but time, son.

                        JOSÉ
Well, you see, Maria's mother and my mother were best friends. They
both came into the United States to work. I was born here, but when
I was four, both our families were deported. Maria was born in
Mexico, but when we came in again a year later, we were deported.
We were told our family could never live legally in the U.S.

                         SISTER GASPAR
Maybe that is true for your parents, but you are an American
citizen, and this is your baby.

                            JOSÉ
                (looks at MARÍA, hesitantly)
Not exactly.

                       SISTER BALTAZAR
Well, that will take some explaining.

                            JOSÉ
Sister, I never touched María. She was pregnant when we married.
The wedding night she put on her gown, and I saw it right away. I
was angry, and she started crying and told me an angel came to her
and told her God would give her a child.
                (to self)
An angel. More like that scumbag Angel Rodriguez who used to brag
about how he could get any girl—

                       SISTER BALTAZAR
Let's keep focused.

                            JOSÉ
Sorry, sister. Anyway, I was going to kick María out. It was hard,
you know? I loved her all my life. She and my moms are tight, you
know? But the next night I have a dream, and in the dream an angel
comes - a real angel - not that pendejo Angel. And this angel said I
should accept María and her child, so I did, but María's reputation
in our town was going to be ruined. You know, people can count.
They would know this wasn't my baby. I didn't want him to grow up
the town bastard with me as the dope who got tricked and María a
fallen woman. I knew we would have no life there. So we came here.
But she has no papers.

                (The baby starts crying.)

                       SISTER MELCORA
Well, this will all work out. Let me check this little one out first.
He sounds hungry. Have you tried to nurse yet?

                           MARÍA
No.

                         SISTER MELCORA
Well, we will work on that.
                    (She picks up the baby and brings
                    him to MARÍA. She takes him in her
                    arms.)
So what are you going to call him?

                              JOSÉ
Call him?

                         SISTER MELCORA
His name. What name will you give him?

                    (JOSÉ and MARíA look at each other.)

                              JOSÉ
Jesús.

                         (BLACKOUT)

                         (END OF PLAY)

DIWALI AND THE OTHER ONES

_____

A Play in One Act

by

Maximillian Gill

<u>Cast of Characters</u>

<u>Kavita</u>:   Female, late 20s, Indian

<u>Manoj</u>:   Male, early 30s, Indian

<u>SCENE</u>
Apartment in a Californian suburb

<u>TIME</u>
1970s

SETTING: Dining room of an apartment.

AT RISE: MANOJ has just returned home from work.
                            KAVITA has been preparing dinner.

MANOJ
The car is making the noise again.

KAVITA
Noise?

MANOJ
The engine. Rattling, knocking. I'll have to take it to the
mechanic.

KAVITA
He repaired it last time.

MANOJ
I think he overcharged me. But what can I do? And gas is going up.
Do you know what a stupid fellow at work asked me? He said "why do
you people keep raising the price of oil?"

KAVITA
He said that?

MANOJ
As if I'm a rich Arab.

KAVITA
They think we're all the same.

MANOJ
And he drives a new Corvette.

KAVITA
I can make chapatis if you're ready to eat.

MANOJ
Sure. What is that tree in the living room?

KAVITA
A Christmas tree.

                         MANOJ
     Christmas?

                         KAVITA
     Akash and I got it today.

                         MANOJ
     How much?

                         KAVITA
     Not too much.

                         MANOJ
     But how much?

                         KAVITA
     It's a small tree. On sale.

                         MANOJ
     And how much are the lights?

                         KAVITA
     A neighbor gave them to me.

                         MANOJ
     Someone gave you lights?

                         KAVITA
     For Akash.

                         MANOJ
     Akash doesn't know about Christmas.

                         KAVITA
     He's heard about it.

                         MANOJ
     You told him?

                         KAVITA
     He goes to school. The children talk about these things.

                         MANOJ
     You want to celebrate Christmas?

KAVITA

What is celebrating? We have a tree.

MANOJ

We didn't even have Diwali this year.

KAVITA

Nobody has Diwali here.

MANOJ

So no Diwali, but Christmas? What would my mother say if she saw a Christmas tree in our home?

KAVITA

She won't see it.

MANOJ

If Akash asks about Santa Claus, I'll have nothing to say.

KAVITA

We just decorate the tree and put some presents under it.

MANOJ

Presents?

KAVITA

Christmas presents.

MANOJ

No. If he wants presents, then no.

KAVITA

People give presents to children.

MANOJ

Where is the money for toys? Did you think about this?

KAVITA

Shh. Keep your voice down. He's napping.

MANOJ

You have no idea, Kavita. The rent, groceries. How do I pay the mechanic? Now you want to buy presents?

                         KAVITA
The Salvation Army store has cheap toys.

                         MANOJ
You want to tell him a strange man in red clothes will leave him
presents?

                         KAVITA
He already knows.

                         MANOJ
Do you hear how ridiculous that is?

                         KAVITA
It's just a tree.

                         MANOJ
In our living room.

                         KAVITA
For Diwali we light lamps and make rangoli. What is the sense in
that?

                         MANOJ
That is our tradition.

                         KAVITA
Not anymore.

                         MANOJ
This is too much, Kavita.

                         KAVITA
What are you saying?

                         MANOJ
No presents, no tree.

                         KAVITA
You want me to throw it out?

                         MANOJ
Return it and get back the money.

                    KAVITA
I can't.

                    MANOJ
Then just give it to somebody who wants it.

                    KAVITA
Our son wants it.

                    MANOJ
He doesn't. You're just putting nonsense in his head.

                    KAVITA
It's my fault?

                    MANOJ
You got the tree.

                    KAVITA
Okay, Halloween. Do you know it?

                    MANOJ
What, Halloween?

                    KAVITA
Yes, in October.

                    MANOJ
Why do I care?

                    KAVITA
Akash was the only child in his school without a costume.

                    MANOJ
Costume.

                    KAVITA
They dress up.

                    MANOJ
I know what they do.

                    KAVITA
Children knocked on our door for candy. I didn't have any.

                    MANOJ
They should stay away.

                    KAVITA
Akash cried.

                    MANOJ
He what?

                    KAVITA
He said they did a parade in school. He was the only one not in a
costume. The other ones laughed and asked what he was dressed as.
His teacher said he was dressed as...

                    MANOJ
What?

                    KAVITA
A little boy from a place very far away.

                    MANOJ
Okay, so that's what he is.

                    KAVITA
I promised him a costume next year.

                    MANOJ
A little boy is good enough.

                    KAVITA
What?

                    MANOJ
He's a little boy. He doesn't need a costume.

                    KAVITA
You don't want that tree?

                    MANOJ
I don't.

                    KAVITA
Then you tell him.

MANOJ

I'll do it now.

KAVITA

Wait until he wakes up.

MANOJ

You'll see. He doesn't care about these things.

KAVITA

He helped me choose it. I put up the lights after he fell asleep.
As a surprise.

MANOJ

You watch.

KAVITA

First, you look at this.

(She hands him a piece of paper with
a drawing.)

MANOJ

What is it?

KAVITA

A Christmas tree.

MANOJ

This is a tree?

KAVITA

He's five years old.

MANOJ

He draws.

KAVITA

You see this at the bottom.

MANOJ

"For Daddy."

KAVITA

He worked so hard to get the letters perfect.

                    MANOJ
My son likes to draw.

                    KAVITA
He's good at it.

                    MANOJ
I hope he's good at math too.

                    KAVITA
What?

                    MANOJ
Drawing trees won't get him a job.

                    KAVITA
You will thank him for this.

                    MANOJ
Sure.

                    KAVITA
No, you will say "thank you, son, for this beautiful drawing."

                    MANOJ
Yes, fine.

                    KAVITA
And then you'll take that tree away from him?

                    MANOJ
It's the right thing to do.

                    KAVITA
You want to see him cry?

                    MANOJ
He will get over it.

                    KAVITA
Why does it bother you so much?

                    MANOJ
I don't know why you don't understand. These things are not ours.
They are theirs.

KAVITA

Who?

MANOJ

My stupid co-workers who don't even know where I'm from, can't
pronounce my name. They laugh at my accent. That tree is theirs.
It's not who we are.

KAVITA

Who are we, Manoj? Huh?

MANOJ

You don't even know anymore, do you?

KAVITA

They do these things here.

MANOJ

So?

KAVITA

If we want to be here, we have to do them too.

MANOJ

You want to be one of them.

KAVITA

What else do I do?

MANOJ

Do you think they will ever accept you?

KAVITA

I have to try.

MANOJ

I don't even know how to talk to you anymore.

KAVITA

We are keeping the tree.

MANOJ

I'll throw it in the garbage.

KAVITA

I'll get another one.

                    MANOJ
You don't have money.

                    KAVITA
We will have a tree in our home.

                    MANOJ
Fine.

                    KAVITA
I'm serious.

                    MANOJ
I remember. I remember my mother making these beautiful rangoli
designs and I had to step around them so carefully. I couldn't
believe she could make them out of just colored powder. And the
lights. In the village we had rows of lamps outside every house.
All along the street. The fireworks. I had to keep my hands over
my ears but I loved looking at them. And of course we could eat
sweets. So many. My favorite was always gulab jamun coated with
silver leaf. That's not good enough for Akash?

                    KAVITA
I didn't know you cared so much about Diwali.

                    MANOJ
It's something I lost.

                    KAVITA
I lost things too.

                    MANOJ
You don't act like it.

                    KAVITA
We can make lamps. Maybe even sweets. Next year.

                    MANOJ
No reason to.

                    KAVITA
But we will celebrate the other ones too.

                    MANOJ
That's who we are now?

                         KAVITA
We are a family.

                         MANOJ
American family or Indian family?

                         KAVITA
Shh, I hear him, he's up.

                         AKASH
              (offstage)
Mummy, daddy, the tree has lights! So pretty.

                    (BLACKOUT)

                    (END OF PLAY)

JOYEUX NOEL:
AN EXISTENTIAL CHRISTMAS

A Play in One Act

by

James McLindon

<u>Cast of Characters</u>

<u>Head Elf</u>:	30s to 60s, female elf
<u>Flurry</u>:	20s, female elf
<u>Wintry Mix</u>:	20s, male elf
<u>Emile</u>:	20s, male elf, French

<u>SCENE</u>
Santa's workshop

<u>TIME</u>
Almost Christmas Eve

SETTING: Santa's workshop

AT RISE: ELVES stand at a workbench in Santa's
                                  workshop making dolls. They are all as
                                  happy and smiley as can be, singing "Up on
                                  the House Top". The HEAD ELF is a middle-
                                  aged female elf, perhaps a bit rotund,
                                  but with an air of authority. WINTRY MIX,
                                  a male elf, is younger, as is FLURRY, a
                                  female elf. In walks EMILE, his face a
                                  mix of Gallic disdain and despair. All
                                  are dressed as elves, save that EMILE
                                  sports a black beret instead of a cap.
                                  He speaks, with a Parisian accent, from
                                  a profoundly tortured soul, with a dash
                                  of contempt for anyone not intelligent
                                  enough to be despairing with him. He is,
                                  if not handsome, at least existentially
                                  sexy.

                                  ELVES
*Up on the house top, reindeer pause. Out jumps good old Santa
Claus. Down through the chimney with lots of toys. All for the
little ones' Christmas joys. Oh ho ho, who wouldn't go?*

                    (One by one, they spot EMILE. Something
                    about his soul-aching aspect makes
                    each stop singing.)

                                  HEAD ELF
Oh...hello.

                                  EMILE
Is this that which is called "the workshop"?

                                  HEAD ELF
Why, yes, it is. You must be the new elf. Welcome!

                           FLURRY and WINTRY MIX
Welcome!

                    (They all beam at EMILE in an awkward
                    silence. EMILE takes them in, one by
                    one, then sighs despondently.)

                    HEAD ELF
And what might your name be?
                    (EMILE walks slowly toward the bench.
                    The ELVES look at each other, puzzled.)
Elf?

                    EMILE
You ask who I am. Who are you? Who are any of us...in the end: no
one.

                    HEAD ELF
Well...actually, I'm the Head Elf! Welcome!

               FLURRY and WINTRY MIX
Welcome!

                    EMILE
Welcome is the father of farewell, itself the beaten stepchild of
loss.

                    FLURRY
                (to the ELVES)
I ... think he's just a little shy.
                (to EMILE)
Don't be shy! I'm called Flurry!

                    EMILE
                (moving too close to FLURRY)
I am not.

                    FLURRY
                (flustered)
Called Flurry? No, boy, that would be some coincidence—
                (stepping back)
Oh, you mean you're not shy! Gosh, shut up, Flurry.

                    EMILE
Never stull your own voice. Death will do that soon enough.

                    FLURRY
Steal my own voice? Or still it?

                    EMILE
Stull it.

                    FLURRY
             (confused)
...okay.

                    EMILE
I am called Emile. Pronounced ay-meal-luh.

                    WINTRY MIX
Amelia?

                    EMILE
Emile.

                    FLURRY
Emily.

                    EMILE
Emile.

                    HEAD ELF
Emmett?

                    EMILE
Emi—

                    HEAD ELF
How about we call you Mike?

                    WINTRY MIX
You can sit with Flurry and me, Mike! I'm Wintry Mix!
             (offering his hand to shake)
All the other good snow names were taken.

       (EMILE turns away and takes a seat.)

                    FLURRY
So, today, we're making jolly dolls for little girls!

                    WINTRY MIX
Each one is prettier than the last!

                    FLURRY
It's going to be the best Christmas ever—

                    EMILE
It is necessary that I now have my cigarette.
                    (A stunned pause, then all the ELVES
                    laugh their jolliest laughs until
                    EMILE produces a cigarette. He taps it
                    on the work bench to pack the tobacco.
                    The others are horrified, gazing at
                    the cigarette like it's the devil.)
Is it that you have for me a light?

                    FLURRY AND WINTRY MIX
No.

                    HEAD ELF
I'm afraid there's no smoking here.

                    EMILE
                    (a long sigh)
Where then is the room of breaks?

                    HEAD ELF
The wha—oh, the break room? We don't have one. No one takes breaks
here. You see, we're jolly elves!

                    EMILE
Who toil endlessly until death enfolds you in his sweet embrace.

                    WINTRY MIX
Not...really? We make toys that delight children the world over!

                    EMILE
Children who will soon join this weary race around the sun for
a few short years until they become dust like their mothers and
fathers, and for what?

                    FLURRY
Well...but they'll have children, and—

                    EMILE
And the pointless dance begins again.

                    HEAD ELF
The North Pole is made out of wood, Mike. So, no smoking.

                    EMILE
I am called Emile.

                    WINTRY MIX
The only fires permitted are in the jolly fireplaces that banish
winter's chill.

                    EMILE
And these fireplaces...can they banish also the chill of despair?

                    HEAD ELF
That's not very jolly.

                    EMILE
Oh, but death, _he_ is very jolly. He laughs his fill at us. And yet
we fear him so. When the exhausted traveler should long for his
destination.

                    FLURRY
It's just...smoking can kill you.

                    EMILE
Life will kill you. Life is fatal, and yet, you choose to live.

                    (A troubling pause as all ponder
                    this.)

                    HEAD ELF
Well...come on now, everyone. Back to work on the...the jolly
dolls. Christmas is coming!

                    EMILE
                    (picking up some dolls)
All of these dolls are smiling.

                    HEAD ELF
Yes! Aren't they jolly?!

                    EMILE
But women do not always smile.
                    (EMILE walks over to FLURRY, standing
                    too close. FLURRY takes a half-step
                    back.)
For inside all women lies a deep and secret sorrow.

                         FLURRY
                (looking at her chest as if to see
                her soul)
It does?

                         HEAD ELF
But...that's just how dolls look.

                (The other ELVES nod and murmur
                assent, unsure what EMILE is driving
                at.)

                         FLURRY
But Mike's right. That's not how all girls look.

                         HEAD ELF
Well, it's how all girls want to look and how they want their dolls
to look. It makes them feel jolly!

                         EMILE
Happiness is just the pretty veil that they wear...

                         HEAD ELF
Exactly!

                         EMILE
Over the specter of their grief.

                         HEAD ELF
What? No, no grief! There's no grief at Christmas!

                         EMILE
Christmas celebrates the birth of a beautiful child.

                         HEAD ELF
Exactly—

                         EMILE
Who is born only to be hideously mutilated and murdered. A human
sacrifice for which we are all, each of us, to blame.

                         WINTRY MIX
No.

                         EMILE
Christmas is about grief. Sadness. Pain.

                         HEAD ELF
No.

                          EMILE
Loss.

                         FLURRY
No.

                          EMILE
Regret.

                        WINTRY MIX
Stop it.

                          EMILE
Death.

               (A stunned pause. WINTRY MIX buries
               his face in the HEAD ELF's shoulder.

                         FLURRY
                   (stepping forward)
Mike is—

                          EMILE
Emile.

                         FLURRY
Emmett is right. We should make toys that are like real life.

                  HEAD ELF and WINTRY MIX
                     (horrified)
What?

                         FLURRY
Well, why not?

                          EMILE
Because the Head Elf is also correct. Man does not want truth. Man
prefers dreams.

                         HEAD ELF
I said that?

                              EMILE
But truth is what Man needs. I will start a new workshop. The
workshop of truth. That will make true toys. For true children.

                             FLURRY
Does that mean no dolls?

                              EMILE
We will make true dolls, dressed in dreary rags in which they labor
ceaselessly, for no purpose, until death's tender kiss.

                           WINTRY MIX
Can they maybe be jolly rags, at least?

                            HEAD ELF
And you'll still make jolly red wagons for boys, right?

                              EMILE
Our wagons will be made of black, splintered wood and broken axles
to teach the futility of endeavor, the cruelty of a life that
conspires against the fulfillment of our simplest hopes...who is
brave enough to join me?
              (WINTRY MIX bursts into tears.)
Not you. Head Elf?

                            HEAD ELF
No. Never! For you...you are evil!

                              EMILE
              (approaching FLURRY closely)
Flurry?
              (holding out his hand)
Will you join me?
              (extending hand past her)
Together, we can be—

                             FLURRY
              (reaching behind her back to take
              his hand)
We can be a candle in the darkness of life's despair. A candle that
draws souls to us for comfort.

                              EMILE
...no. We will be the snuffer that euthanizes the candle's dying
flame. Together, we will extinguish the lying fire with the truth of
darkness, sadness and death.

                    FLURRY
              (enraptured by him)
Okay.

                    EMILE
Farewell. We leave you alone and friendless in this dusk that you
foolishly mistake for dawn.

          (FLURRY and EMILE leave. WINTRY MIX
          and HEAD ELF watch, stunned.)

                  WINTRY MIX
We're not really alone. And friendless. Are we, Head Elf?

                   HEAD ELF
I think he's just a little...depressed, Wintry Mix.

                  WINTRY MIX
What's "depressed" mean?

                   HEAD ELF
Never mind. Come on! Let's get back to our jolly work!

                  WINTRY MIX
Okay!

              (They begin to make dolls again.
              WINTRY MIX and then HEAD ELF begin
              to sing Up On The House Top in their
              jolly manner.)

                   HEAD ELF
Up on the house top, reindeer pause...

              HEAD ELF and WINTRY MIX
Out jumps good old Santa Claus...
              (WINTRY MIX is his old self, but
              HEAD ELF begins to look troubled,
              and as the song progresses, falls
              behind WINTRY MIX in the singing,
              her voice trailing off. She stares
              out over the crowd, the 1000-yard
              stare.)
*Down through the chimney with lots of toys. All for the little
ones' Christmas joys...*

(HEAD ELF stops singing.)

                    WINTRY MIX
Hey, c'mon, Head Elf: sing with me!
          (HEAD ELF continues to stare out
          over the audience, deeply troubled.)
All for the little ones' Christmas joys—

          (HEAD ELF makes eye contact with
          the audience. She speaks with soul-
          killing despair.)

                    HEAD ELF
Are there any Christmas joys in this vale of tears?

                    WINTRY MIX
Yes!
          (beginning to doubt)
Aren't there?
          (HEAD ELF drops her tools, picks up
          EMILE's discarded cigarette, and
          puts it in her mouth. The sound of a
          howling wind as HEAD ELF exits.)
Head Elf, aren't there?!
          (turning to us for comfort and
          support)
Aren't there?!

          (WINTRY MIX gazes at us in desperation.
          Lost in our own despairing trudge to
          annihilation, we have none to offer.)

               (BLACKOUT)

               (END OF PLAY)

GHOST OF UNION STATION

A Play in One Act

by

Mark Sbani

<u>Cast of Characters</u>

<u>Leo Perino</u>:   54, a security guard

<u>Rose Lipstein</u>:   35, a housewife

<u>Radio Host</u>:   Narrator

<u>SCENE</u>
Union Station, Denver, Colorado

<u>TIME</u>
Halloween, 1949 & 2025

SETTING: The basement of Union Station.

AT RISE: "Night on Bald Mountain" by Modest
                            Mussorgsky plays and soon fades. This
                            will be a recurring interlude throughout
                            the play. A person enters stage left and
                            stands in the middle of the stage under
                            spotlight——the RADIO HOST.

                          RADIO HOST
Welcome, everyone, to the Union Station Radio Show! Thanks for
joining me on this fine evening.
                 (sounds of applause)
Our performance is being recorded live at Union Station, on 17th
Avenue, in downtown Denver. I love bare mountain air, don't you?
                 (sounds of train whistles, then
                 rumbles through)
So good to be with you from this modernized lobby. I'm the host of
tonight's broadcast.
                 (A musical interlude plays for ten
                 seconds.)
Right on, right on. We're going to memory lane it now——tell a story
of Old Denver and reveal the secret history of Union Station. I
promise to bring you a spooky-dooky Halloween. Oh, there will be a
beautiful woman in distress, an unsuspecting guard, and mini-mole
people. Yes!
                 (sounds of mole people chatter)
Mini-mole people! Pocket-sized! They spy on Rose and Leo from the
lower depths of Union Station. Just wait and listen. We're living
in the 2020s, but mentally time travel back to the 1940s. Yeah,
it's the '40s. That's right. Nineteen fourty-nine, in fact. The
Second World War is over. Denver City is booming. Ten-thousand
people a day travel through Union Station. Now let's go down deep
into the basement. Ah yeah, under the rails.
                 (a mock villainous laugh)
It's time to kick off the show! A seasonal production of Mark
Sbani's "Ghost of Union Station."

                 (RADIO HOST takes their seat out of
                 the spotlight as the musical interlude
                 plays for ten seconds.)

                          ROSE
Ssst! Are you the night watchman?

                    LEO
               (distracted)
Oh, I didn't see you there. You snuck up on me. Hello, I'm Officer
Leo Perino. What's your name?

                    ROSE
Rose Lipstein.

                    LEO
Rose, how can I help you?

                    ROSE
Please, come a little closer. Get over here.

                    LEO
Ma'am, the platform's this way. Up the stairs.

                    ROSE
They cancelled it. The midnight service to Black Hawk. A tunnel
closed. Or thick fog.

                    LEO
So you came down here, why?

                    ROSE
               (very quietly)
I heard something: voices. Drunken hobos, screaming at each other.

                    LEO
You heard voices in the basement?

                    ROSE
Transients. When I turned the corner, they vanished. They went
poof! Now look for the trespassers, Officer Perino. Duty calls.

                    LEO
Nobody's allowed in this area. It's restricted. Been closed all
year, due to a wrongful death.

                    ROSE
Did you say "Due to wrongful death?" That's significant.

                         LEO
How so?

                         ROSE
Well, someone died, didn't they? On your watch. Are you even paying
attention? You're giving me cow eyes.

                         LEO
Look, I'm just going to say this. Whatever happened, it happened
one year ago, tonight.
                    (sounds of heavy footsteps)
Alright, well, I don't see anything. No unusual activity. Twenty-
three-forty-five on October 31st, 1949. Let's go back upstairs, huh?

                         ROSE
I can't. My husband Ed is waiting for me in the lobby. Ed thinks I
wronged him. That I two-timed him with his bowling buddy, so I'm
hiding. Hiding from Ed. He is an insanely jealous man. I walked out
on him, but he followed me here. Down to the tracks. His name is Ed
Rossi, Officer. Put that in your report. Ed Rossi.

                         LEO
Eddie Spaghetti. With ravioli eyes and a meatball head.

                         ROSE
You kind of look like him, you know. You're both skinny Italians.

                         LEO
As a matter of fact, I'm full-blooded Italian. Four-fourths.

                         ROSE
Andiamo, Leo. Andiamo. Let's go. Move it.

                         LEO
Look, all I see are black walls and you—an insurance liability.

                         ROSE
What are you worried about? Fraternizing with the public? Huh, Ed?
I mean, Leo.

                         LEO
Of course not. That's against protocol.

                    (musical interlude plays)

                          ROSE
                      (delighted)
Oooh! Devilish music on a Saturday night.

                          LEO
Where the hell is that coming from? Who's really down here?

                          ROSE
Well, Leo, if you go looking, you'll find it.
                    (musical interlude plays)
Do you ride the lines often?

                          LEO
Never.

                          ROSE
Never? I mean, not even once?

                    (music stops)

                          LEO
No. I prefer to use my own two feet. I'm prone to train sickness,
you know. All that bouncing around? While you're eating a meal? No!

                          ROSE
Come this way. Quick.

                          LEO
Where? Where are we going? We're halfway to Black Hawk, Rose.

                          ROSE
Goddamn Union Station. They cancelled Black Hawk. I'll never board
that train.

                          LEO
Rose, tell me about your husband. Ed. Talk more about him.

                          ROSE
                      (softly)
He put me in my grave and left me there.
                      (loudly)
Now investigate! Patrol, guard, patrol!

                    LEO
I'm always on patrol. I don't know how to sit down.
                (sounds of footsteps)
Mm, maybe I should investigate you. You said you left your husband,
but where's your luggage? You heard voices. What, unbodied voices?
Are they real or are they a diversion?

                    ROSE
Exactly what are you suggesting?

                    LEO
That I need to report back. It's time to turn in the keys. I'm sorry.
                (cackles and snarls)
You hear that? Shhh! Listen! That's them, in the distance.

                    ROSE
Who?

                    LEO
Mole people.

                    ROSE
                (in disbelief)
Are you serious? Mole people?

                    LEO
Dennis—my relieving officer—he saw them and passed down the
information. Description: pink eyes, phosphorescent skin. Miniature
humans who live underground. They hunt in packs. Little devils.
They're watching us right now. I mean it. We're in real danger.

                    ROSE
Leo, your hands are shaking. Are you all right?

                    LEO
No, I'm petrified with fear.

                    ROSE
Hey, let's do something heroic. Let's detain them.
                (more cackles)
You got a Union Station issued whistle, Leo, use it.
                (whistle blows)
That's right! Blow it again.

(A whistle blows twice.)

                    LEO
Please stand back, Rose. A commuter railroad can be a dangerous
environment. You ride at your own risk.

                    ROSE
Oh, I'm not afraid. Are you, Ed?

                    LEO
You seem to forget my name. I'm Leo Perino. Strange, very strange.
Calling me by your husband's name.

                    ROSE
Leo, turn around.

                    LEO
Why? Why are you so interested in me?

                    ROSE
I like you. I'm sorry.

                    LEO
But I don't understand why.

                    ROSE
I apologize. I suppose you hate me.

                    LEO
No, I just don't trust you. I never trust beautiful women.

                    ROSE
You don't?

                    LEO
And your name. You see, I'm allergic to roses. The flowers. Any
color, under my nose, I get what's called rose fever.

                    RADIO HOST
                (in a distorted voice)
Attention! This is a security announcement. We ask you to avoid eye
contact with the transients. Their mood has become dark. If you see
something that isn't right, page the night watchman, Officer Leo
Perino. He'll sort it out.

                         ROSE
You hear that, Ed? Sort it out.

                         LEO
Are you talking to me?

              (sounds of a train passing overhead)

                         ROSE
Eddddddd!

                         LEO
Fine. Call me anything you want.

                         ROSE
Oh, what's this? An old baggage car, huh? Go on, climb in.

              (a creaky metal door opens)

                         LEO
Oh no. I'm not getting in there. I have a funny feeling.

                         ROSE
                   (whispering)
He lifted me up by the throat and crushed my larynx.

                         LEO
Rose, you speak too softly. I really can't hear you.

                         ROSE
And you speak too loudly. It's quiet in the baggage car.

                      RADIO HOST
                 (in a distorted voice)
Paging Officer Perino! It's quarter to midnight. No one knows where
the watchman is? Leo. Is he lost, or more crucially, is he missed?

                         ROSE
Leo, get in. I don't have time for this. Get inside. Now.
                   (LEO sighs, then climbs inside the
                   baggage car.)
Don't tell me how to live. And don't call me stupid. Or you'll be
sorry, Ed.

                              LEO
I didn't say you were stupid. And I'm not these other men. We've
been through this. I'm a courtly gentleman. Ask anyone.

                              ROSE
                      (bitterly)
You took me into the basement, Ed, then strangled and discarded me.

                              LEO
I never strangled anyone!

                              ROSE
You strangled me with one hand. Grasped my neck and squeezed. My
chin is so small, it was easy. My half-a-chin didn't get in the
way. My ch—

                              LEO
Look, Rose, you're very upset. You have a lot of emotional
problems. I mean, everybody does.

                              ROSE
I don't have emotional problems!

                    (an open-handed slap)

                         RADIO HOST
As I said at the top of the show, she's troubled.

                              LEO
Hey! Are you crazy? You can't hit an officer. That's felonious!
                    (metal door slamming shut, then
                    locking)
Hey, what's the big idea? The door. You slammed it in my face.
                    (knocking on the window)
Open the door, Rose! Open it! Did you lock me in? Rose, I can see
you through the window. You shut me in!

                              ROSE
One year dead. I am one year dead, upon the hour.

                              LEO
Rose, you're not alive?

                              ROSE
Very observant, Leo. I'm a ghost and you disrespected me.

                              LEO
I disrespected you? Leo Perino? That doesn't sound like me.

                              ROSE
Last year, you were working the night shift. You were supposed to
be guarding the lobby.

                              LEO
                    (terrified)
All right, so take my badge. Don't take my life. Please!
                    (sounds of a fist pounding on a metal
                    door)
This is wrong!
                    (furiously)
You don't trap people for no reason.

                              ROSE
You saw me and did nothing. You went limp, as Ed dragged me
downstairs.

                              LEO
I don't remember that.

                              ROSE
                    (lamenting)
Well, I do. Those were my last moments. I died miserably.

                              LEO
I'm sorry. I'm sorry. I wasn't paying attention.

                              ROSE
You get paid to pay attention. It was your duty to respond, Leo.

                              LEO
                    (panic-stricken)
Rose! It was an honest mistake. I learned my lesson. I'll never
fall asleep on post again.

                              ROSE
You let me down, Leo. You owe me.

                              LEO
Owe you what?

                              ROSE
Your life, Ed.

                              LEO
I'm Leo! Leo Perino!

                              ROSE
This is for the ghosts of the past. Hundreds of poor souls failed
by bystanders in Union Station. This is for the cries of help that
went ignored. For all the unemployed under the platform who froze
to death.

                              LEO
My heart is racing. I can't breathe.
                    (fingernails scratching on metal and
                     whimpering)
Rose. Rose!

                              ROSE
Awww, baby blue eyes. If you cry harder, maybe it'll get better.

                              LEO
That's a ghost talking. I'm ignoring her. I don't believe she
exists.

                              ROSE
Oh, Leo. You're such a fool!

                              LEO
You can't just leave me here.

                           RADIO HOST
What a bum-out, Leo. You're locked inside a baggage car,
underground. You're totally fucked.

                              LEO
Rose! I'll arrest you for false imprisonment! What am I talking
about? I'll arrest your husband when I get out of here. I'll charge
him with murder by strangulation.

                              ROSE
Ah! That's the correct answer. Arrest my husband.

                              LEO
Okay, then unlock this door immediately!

ROSE

Here's a clue, detective. You hold the key to your cell.

LEO

Where is my master set? Do I have the baggage key or not?
                    (sound of keys jingling, then the
                    lock turns)
It fits. I'm free! Oh Lord, thank you! I'm loving life!
                    (metal door opening)
Rose? Rose? Are you there?

ROSE

Well, Leo, I'd love to stay and chitchat, but I'm leaving. My train
is pulling out.

RADIO HOST
                    (in a distorted voice)
May I have your attention. The midnight train to Black Hawk is
back in service. The fog has dissipated, allowing us to see things
clearly. All aboard! Boarding.
                    (prolonged applause with spotlight
                    on RADIO HOST)
Thank you very much. We really appreciate that. Okay, ladies and
gentlemen, that's our program. This production was brought to you
by friends at the Union Station Radio Show. Happy Halloween, people.

                    (sound of villainous laughter)

                              (BLACKOUT)

                              (END OF PLAY)

SSEKUKULU (CHRISTMAS)
_____

A Play in One Act

by

Achiro P. Olwoch

Cast of Characters

Davis: Lightskin black male, Shamba boy.
                                Walks like he owns the compound.

Comfort: Black female, early 20s with an
                                afro or swahili lines in her hair.
                                Dark skin and very bubbly. Wears
                                an apron over her dress. House
                                help.

SCENE
Ugandan home

TIME
Christmas Day in Uganda, Present day

SETTING: Large suburban house surrounded by a wall
                             fence. Back door verandah. Four dog
                             kennels out front. Ten in the morning.

AT RISE: COMFORT and DAVIS sit outside having
                             breakfast.

                          DAVIS
I love Ssekukulu.

                          COMFORT
I hate it.

                          DAVIS
Why? All the booze and food Bwana gives us.

                          COMFORT
That's exactly the same reason I hate it.

                          DAVIS
But you get to eat as much as you can serve yourself.

                          COMFORT
Guess who does the washing up and cleaning afterwards?

                          DAVIS
So you have to wash a few plates.

                          COMFORT
A few? Bwana's whole family comes over and sometimes even Madam
invites hers. Those children are so messy.

                          DAVIS
Make them clean up their messes.

                          COMFORT
Madam says it's <u>my</u> job.

                          DAVIS
I can understand that if it's just the four kids, but during
Ssekukulu, it's fourteen. Plus the eight adults.

                          COMFORT
It's just too much work.

                         DAVIS
Would you rather prepare the chickens and goat?

                        COMFORT
Oh, this Ssekukulu you will prepare a pig and a goat.

                         DAVIS
You lie. I have been presented a goat and eight chickens to
slaughter.

                        COMFORT
Bwana's brother has gone out to buy the pig.

                         DAVIS
A whole pig?

                        COMFORT
If you can prepare a goat, you can prepare a pig.

                         DAVIS
It's not the same process. Pigs are tricky. I hope he brings it
dead.

                        COMFORT
He is buying it for New Year. It will be very much alive.

                         DAVIS
But why?

                        COMFORT
You should ask him.

                         DAVIS
You know I can't just approach the Bwana like that.

                        COMFORT
Bwana's brother is kind. You can tell him anything.

                         DAVIS
That's true.

                        COMFORT
He is the only one who thanks us with extra cash at the end of
Ssekukulu.

                         DAVIS
I love his cash bonuses.

                         COMFORT
Like I said, he is a kind man.

                         DAVIS
But he has already gone out to buy the pig.

                         COMFORT
Did you open the gate for him?

                         DAVIS
Not yet.

                         COMFORT
Then he hasn't left yet.

                         DAVIS
But how do I start?

                         COMFORT
Suggest he buys a dead pig. We can keep it in the freezer.

                         DAVIS
There is no space in the freezer.

                         COMFORT
We will make space.

                         DAVIS
For a whole pig?

                         COMFORT
Would you rather slaughter a fresh one on the day?

                         DAVIS
...we will make space.

                         COMFORT
Now you see why I hate Ssekukulu.

                         DAVIS
I am starting to hate it too.

                         COMFORT
Remember all the booze.

                         DAVIS
Ah, yes, and now I love it all over again.

                              COMFORT
We should get back to work.

                              DAVIS
Hapana. I have just finished cleaning up all the five dogs' poop from
the night. Those dogs eat too much. I am tired.

                              COMFORT
Is that why you starve them?

                              DAVIS
I don't starve them.

                              COMFORT
Davis, I have seen you prepare their food. You put very little flour
to make their porridge.

                              DAVIS
That's not meant to starve them.

                              COMFORT
What then?

                              DAVIS
Using little flour spreads it out, and I can lie to the Madam that
the flour is finished. She never checks for herself. Then she gives
me money and just like that, I have pocket money to spend.

                              COMFORT
That's evil, Davis.

                              DAVIS
It is called entrepreneurship.

                              COMFORT
Don't let Bwana see you make that thin porridge.

                              DAVIS
Haven't you noticed I make it and feed the dogs just before he gets
back from work.

                              COMFORT
Be careful. That man loves his dogs more than he loves his children.

                              DAVIS
That's the truth.

COMFORT

Do you know he greets them first every morning and when he gets back before he even enters the house.

DAVIS

I have seen that. Makes me laugh each time.

COMFORT

Like I said, Bwana loves his dogs.

DAVIS

He found me once making that light porridge and threatened to fire me.

COMFORT

You know they can never let you go.

DAVIS

I know. He owes my father a favor that's why he keeps me.

COMFORT

You have never told me that story properly.

DAVIS

Well, it's a simple story really. You know how Bwana used to work upcountry in my village?

COMFORT

He was the district commissioner, he didn't work in your village, Davis.

DAVIS

My home district is my village. Anyway, there was a plot to poison him by his colleagues. They didn't appreciate that a man from another tribe was head of their office. My father was the gate keeper, and he warned him. Long story short, he got rid of his enemies and owed my father. So here I am.

COMFORT

It doesn't mean you should take advantage of his kindness.

DAVIS

I just do what I need to survive.

COMFORT

If you starve those dogs to death, there is nothing that will let him keep you on.

                         DAVIS
        I give them just enough. They will be fine.

                         COMFORT
        Also, one day those dogs will rebel and eat you instead.

                         DAVIS
        Those dogs love me.

                         COMFORT
        People hurt the ones they love.

                         DAVIS
        Then we should thank the good Lord they are not people.

                         COMFORT
        You know what I mean.

                         DAVIS
        I know...so, what is in store for you today?

                         COMFORT
        Eh, don't remind me. I woke up at 4am to clean the house before
        anyone was awake. Then I set out to make breakfast, now I am doing
        the laundry.

                         DAVIS
        Same as every day, then.

                         COMFORT
        Yes, when they wake up, I will go make their beds and clean the
        rooms.

                         DAVIS
        Yoh, it's a good thing they pay extra during Ssekukulu.

                         COMFORT
        Only reason I don't take leave to celebrate with my family.

                         DAVIS
        But twelve bedrooms and eight bathrooms? That's a lot of scrubbing
        and cleaning.

                         COMFORT
        The price of working in rich people's mansions.

DAVIS

Sometimes I wish I was working inside the house.

COMFORT

But you get a taste when I take leave.

DAVIS

Yes, but I hate it. It's too much work.

COMFORT

You are paid extra.

DAVIS

It's not enough. I prefer working outside in my own time.

COMFORT

Speaking of time, when are you going to start killing those animals?

DAVIS

As soon as the house wakes up.

COMFORT

Smart man.

DAVIS

I want them to notice that I am working.

COMFORT

You should get the lawn mower then.

DAVIS

Wah, I did that once and Bwana almost put my head under it.

COMFORT

I laughed so hard that day. I mean mowing at 5am, surely Davis?

DAVIS

I was still drunk. I didn't know it was that early.

COMFORT

They all jumped out of bed like there was a bomb threat.

DAVIS

Madam gave me death stares that whole day.

                    COMFORT
It was the weekend and we all know how she loves her beauty sleep.

                    DAVIS
Should I get the mower now?

                    COMFORT
Hapana. Let them sleep. The world is so peaceful while they are
asleep.

                    DAVIS
I know what you mean.

                    COMFORT
Let's enjoy it. When we start working there will be no sitting down
until lunch.

                    DAVIS
And with all the cooking and roasting, lunch will be late.

                    COMFORT
All the washing and cooking is making my head spin.

                    DAVIS
They offered to get you a helper for Ssekukulu and you refused.

                    COMFORT
If they brought a second person they wouldn't pay me as much as
they are, so...

                    DAVIS
How much do they pay you during this period?

                    COMFORT
Enough for me to refuse a helping hand.

                    DAVIS
That much?

                    COMFORT
Imagine how much and multiply that by two.

                    DAVIS
Eh, that much?

                         COMFORT
That much!

                          DAVIS
Now I <u>am</u> jealous.

                         COMFORT
Want to exchange jobs for the day?

                          DAVIS
Ah, no thank you.

                         COMFORT
What irritates me the most is the kids leaving messes every two
seconds. I mean preparations is not too bad because all the Bwanas
and their wives do that. All I have to do is wash and clean up after
them.

                          DAVIS
Why don't they come and help me kill the chickens? Or at least
pluck the feathers when I've killed them.

                         COMFORT
Ask the kids to help.

                          DAVIS
The girls squeal as if the dead chickens have bitten them. Then
they smell their hands all the time and say, 'oh gross' as if those
of us doing it are not present. Then the boys complain about the hot
water as if they would be able to pluck the feathers if the water
was cold. I tell you, these summer children!

                         COMFORT
Spoiled.

                          DAVIS
They are used to seeing dead chicken come from the market.

                         COMFORT
How do they think it gets there?

                          DAVIS
A machine?

                         COMFORT
It's good to be rich.

                    DAVIS
I like the kids. They teach me American English.

                    COMFORT
I can't understand them half the time. I just smile and nod my head.

                    DAVIS
I should get the mower.

                    COMFORT
And wake all twenty people at the same time. Hapana.

                    DAVIS
I am bored.

                    COMFORT
Sweep the compound. Light the sigiri so you can start boiling the
water for your animals.

                    DAVIS
I thought you'd boil it for me.

                    COMFORT
No, I have too much work of my own.

                    DAVIS
Oba, I start with the goat?

                    COMFORT
The whole goat will be barbecued in the evening. There is frozen
goat meat, pork, fish and beef for lunch in the freezer.

                    DAVIS
Again, I love Ssekukulu.

                    COMFORT
Don't make me slap you with a chicken.

                    (BLACKOUT)

                    (END OF PLAY)

ABUELITA LIKES BLUE
_____

A Play in One Act

by

Sofía Méndez Ramírez

Cast of Characters

Ana: Latin woman, 30-45, mother.

Armando: Latin boy, 10. Ana's son.

Laura: Latin woman, 15-20. Ana's daughter.

Mamá Lupe: Latin woman, 60s. Ana's mother.

Eva: Latin woman, 30-40s. Mamá Lupe's cousin.

SCENES
A kitchen and living room

TIME
Christmas Eve, Present day

<u>ACT I</u>

<u>SCENE 1</u>

SETTING: A bustling kitchen.

AT RISE: ARMANDO and LAURA stand unenthused,
                             chopping vegetables next to a big table.
                             ANA cleans mushrooms next to them, happy.

                    ANA
Mamá Lupe is going to love this.

                    ARMANDO
I don't want to go...

                    ANA
What? Of course you do, my boy. Nadie se queda en casa. It's
Christmas!

                    ARMANDO
You say it as if there was a...
          (adding air quotes)
..."multitude" here. It's just the three of us.

                    ANA
Why don't you want to go? There's going to be delicious food. Eva
is making the arroz con leche you love.

                    LAURA
Mom, you know Eva doesn't cook like abuelita.

                    ARMANDO
That's true. It's not the same.

                    ANA
You guys know Mamá Lupe can't cook anymore. I miss her cooking,
though.

                    ARMANDO
Besides, she doesn't even care if I'm there.

                    ANA
What do you mean? She obviously cares! Why do you say that?

ARMANDO

The last time we went to visit her she told me: "Oh, my dear. You shouldn't disappear like that. You weren't here last Christmas." Like, what? I was there! We played Jenga and sang those stupid songs she likes. She doesn't even notice if I go or not.

ANA

I mean, she doesn't do it on purpose.

LAURA

I don't want to go either, Armando. But here we are, chopping these *stupid* vegetables. I would rather go with Tania and John to see the Christmas light show downtown.

ARMANDO
            (stops chopping)
See? I don't think I have anything like that with abuelita!

ANA

First of all, those stupid vegetables — this recipe is part of my youth, Laura. Don't you remember when you ate celery with abuelita for the first time? And you are not going to the light show. I told you — Christmas is...
            (looking between them)
...family only.

LAURA

They *are* my family.

ANA

Christmas is for the family you grew up with. Period.

ARMANDO

What if she doesn't remember again, next year? That I was there? That won't make a difference. Laura and I can go to the light show.

ANA
            (stops cleaning)
Ok, guys. Stop it.
            (to ARMANDO)
Buddy, did you know that when you get old — very old — there are some things you can't do as well as you used to?

ARMANDO

...like running?

ANA

Yeah. Running is hard y'know? Well, there are some other things that are even harder or get harder...like...do you remember what you ate for breakfast yesterday?

ARMANDO

Molletes with pico.

ANA

Well, that was an easy one. See, I don't remember, and I'm just 45! Sometimes our memory captures one thing instead of others, and that can be because we have a lot of things on our mind. Other times, it's because we are stressed, or when you get older, it's because— it's just age. You can forget certain things and that doesn't mean those are not important for you. It just happens, and for some people, that's a big deal.

ARMANDO

Are you trying to say that it's a big deal for abuelita?

ANA

Yes. It is very hard for her. She can't remember a lot of things, but that's mostly when those things happened a long time ago. She can mix up things like when you are singing Las Mañanitas.

ARMANDO

You're always bothering me with that.

ANA

I mean, most people know the lyrics, but you can get confused and make up words that are not there. The point is—Mamá Lupe might not remember things that happened last Christmas, but when she sees you, she remembers you. She knows you are her grandson. She's fulfilled when she sees you, and seeing you helps her remember other good things we've lived through with her.

ARMANDO

When I see her, I remember Dad. I wish he was here.

LAURA
(holding ARMANDO's hand)

I know. I do too, but sometimes when I see abuelita I also remember all the good stuff, and I imagine I'm spending time with a fragment of Dad, because he really loved her. You are also a wonderful piece of who he used to be. So, what about making new memories with abuelita then? Mom will be happy. We are a small family, and we need to stick together.

                        ANA
And I know it can be hard, especially with these family gatherings,
but you haven't seen her since she fell, and I've been respecting
that decision, but today is different.

                        ARMANDO
But she's gonna be fine. She doesn't need us.

                        ANA
                (handing them a photobook)
She does. She thinks about her son when she sees you. I've been
bringing her pictures from the old photobook.

                        LAURA
Why are you showing her those pictures? Is that bad?

                        ANA
You'll see her, just don't freak out. Recovering from a stroke is
difficult. Please choose one picture and we'll all show her.

                        ARMANDO
Are we going to keep cooking?

                        ANA
Yes, please. Just choose a picture, and once you are done with
those vegetables, we can start frying them. I'll have the salsa
ready.

                        LAURA
                (mumbles to self)
Salsa would've gone well with the light show.

                        ANA
Next year, okay?

                        (BLACKOUT)

                        (END OF SCENE)

ACT I

SCENE 2

SETTING: MAMÁ LUPE's living room.

AT RISE: MAMÁ LUPE and EVA sit molding clay. EVA
                                talks, but MAMÁ LUPE is silent. She smiles
                                a bit when the doorbell rings.

                    EVA
That must be them! I'll be back.
                    (opening the door)
Oh my God, come in! So good to see you, guys. You are getting
taller every time!
                    (LAURA, ANA, and ARMANDO each hug
                    EVA. They enter the living room.)
Lupe, look who came to visit you.
                    (MAMÁ LUPE looks at her
                    grandchildren and smiles. She tries
                    to stand up.)
No, they'll come to you. Kids, please. She can't move right now.
She's just getting worse.

                    ANA
We are hoping she'll recover soon.
                    (to LAURA)
Go ahead, my dear.

                    LAURA
                    (LAURA approaches MAMÁ LUPE, holds
                    her hand, and hugs her.)
Abuelita, how are you doing?
                    (MAMÁ LUPE speaks, but mumbling
                    is heard. LAURA looks at ANA,
                    confused.)
Mom?

                    ARMANDO
Abuelita, can you repeat that?

                    (MAMÁ LUPE tries to talk.)

                         ANA
Mom, you don't need to.
                  (to children)
Guys, can I talk with you for a second?
                  (stepping to the side)
It's been hard for me to accept that we don't know if Mamá Lupe
will be able to talk again, and as I said, her accident was pretty
bad. But she can understand what you are saying—

                         ARMANDO
—we won't listen to abuelita's voice ever again?

                         ANA
I mean, it is hard to understand what she says, but she tries her
best. We need to support her. Just smile when she's trying to talk,
okay?

             (ARMANDO and LAURA nod.)

                         EVA
Well, are you guys ready to start? I figured we can ask for posada
and then arrullar al Niño Dios, but we can partir la piñata first or
maybe the piñata for tomorrow. Are you guys
staying for the night?

                         ANA
We are. I brought some blankets. The posada may be the best way to
go. It depends on how well Mamá Lupe is doing...

                         EVA
Mija, the best way to know is by trying it.

                         ANA
I guess I need to be an example of optimism for them then.
                  (to her children)
Guys! Come, take the Niño Dios, we're going to pedir posada.

                         LAURA
Abuelita, do you want to hold the niño?
                  (MAMÁ LUPE nods, but her face
                  contorts.)
Aquí estoy. Are you okay?
                  (MAMÁ LUPE weakly hums "mm-hmm.")
We're going to sing. I know that's your favorite part. We'll be
the Peregrinos—

ANA
My dear, I think it's better if you sing for the hosts.

LAURA
Sorry, abuelita. I'm going to crush it. I sing the hosts' part
pretty well.

ANA
Eva, do you have the lyrics?

EVA
In my cell. Do you?

ANA
I'll go by memory.

ARMANDO
Well, I don't remember the lyrics.

ANA
Just use your phone. It's a classic song.

ARMANDO
Okay, okay.

          (They gather together.)

ANA
Uno, dos, go! En el nombre del cie-e-e-lo / Os pido po—

ARMANDO
—sa-da-a-a / Pues pucde

ANA and ARMANDO
—Anda-a-a-ar / Mi esposa ama-a-a-da. Mi esposa ama-a-a-da.

LAURA
          (with unnecessary bravado)
Pues pasenle—

ANA
Mija! Keep singing the original version.

LAURA
I know, but my abuelita is tired, and I would rather sing to the
Niño Dios than do this traditional thing. Plus, I'm hungry, and I
want to drink ponche.

                              ARMANDO
Abuelita, would you like to eat arroz con leche?

                               LAURA
Stop it, Armando. She can't speak. Just serve it.

                                EVA
It's okay, Laura. It helps when other people try. Do you guys want
to see the drawings she did?

                               LAURA
She can paint?

                                EVA
Draw, yes. I mean, she's not Miguel Angel Duarte, but that helps
her get relaxed. She made them before the incident, though.

                               LAURA
Oh...

                                ANA
We want to see them, thank you.

                               LAURA
Have you tried to get her to draw again?

                                ANA
I'm sure Eva is doing all she can.

                                EVA
                       (handing them a box)
I am, indeed. You can see all she has drawn here.

                              ARMANDO
I thought we were going to eat.

                                ANA
Don't be rude, and no. Remember, we always wait until midnight.
                    (looking at the drawings)
These are so cute!
                              ARMANDO
But it's Jesus' birthday, I'm sure he'd want it celebrated as early
as possible.

                                ANA
Jesus, Armando. Please.

                         EVA
It's okay. We can always have a snack, so you guys are not that
hungry. Who wants ponche?

                       ARMANDO
Me, please, but I'll help you serve.

              (ARMANDO heads to the kitchen, looking
              for mugs as EVA checks on the ponche.)

                         LAURA
Abuelita, do you remember that story you told us about you and your
brother singing in a contest? I don't remember all the details,
but you and your brother sang in front of an audience, with the
village governor watching, and he gave you a big gold coin as a
reward for participating. Then your teacher—since it happened at
your school—took both coins, just like that. My mom used to get
mad when she heard that story, but I always thought it was funny
because of the way you told it.

                         EVA
It was one of our Lupe's favorite stories, for sure.

                         LAURA
Oh, my...

              (ARMANDO hands out ponche.)

                         ANA
What? What happened?

                         LAURA
I just realized—abuelito used to do that too. He would give us
money if we sang or danced at one of the family gatherings.

                         ANA
Why'd I never notice?

                         LAURA
Was it because of abuelita's story? Or that's something everyone
does in small towns?

                         ANA
I don't know. I've been thinking that I don't actually know much
about my mom. People change over the years, you know? I got all my
answers when I was a kid and never really asked again. I'm not sure
if my mom's favorite color is still blue.

                    LAURA
I...I'm sure abuelita will be able to answer that soon.

                    ANA
I'm not sure. I don't know what she needs, and honestly, I barely
know her well enough to decide how she'd like to handle this
situation.

          (MAMÁ LUPE starts to babble, but no
          one understands.)

                    EVA
Ana, I feel you, but you still have time. And let me tell you—I do
know a lot of stories about your mom that might help you understand
her better. She's here with us, let's enjoy that. What if we all
share those special moments we shared with Lupe?

                    ANA
I love the idea. We brought one picture to show her.

                    EVA
C'mon. C'mon everyone.

          (They all gather around MAMÁ LUPE.)

                    LAURA
Hey, mami! Do you remember that song or kind of story my great-aunt
used to tell Armando and me? Something about hot chocolate and a
cat—

          (MAMÁ LUPE closes her eyes.)

                    ARMANDO
—I know what you're talking about!
          (singing)
Compadrito Pancho, compadrito Pancho.
          (beat)
It's not working, abuelita is sleeping...
          (she opens her eyes)
Forget it, she's back in the game.

                    LAURA
She just woke up with your singing.

                    ARMANDO
Give me a break.

                              EVA
Lupe and I would play all day with the becerros. You should've seen
her—she always had these beautiful curls, and when I told her I
loved them, she'd try to help me comb my hair so we'd look like
twins.

                              ANA
I remember there was a day I came back from school...I was around
15 years old, and she noticed I was very tired, so she massaged my
feet with a homemade cream she made.

                              LAURA
That's so sweet, Mom...I guess she likes plants and things like
that. She made me tea with herbs from our garden, once I told her I
was sick.

                              ARMANDO
Okay, but she bought me a toy once. I'd asked Mom to buy it for me,
and she said no, but abuelita was there, and the next week we came
to see her, she gave it to me. I was five.

                              LAURA
It seems abuelita has a favorite, huh?

                              ARMANDO
                    (to MAMÁ LUPE)
Abuelita, we brought this picture. Do you remember that day? It was
your birthday and da-

                              LAURA
—Dad brought you serenata. We were making pan de muerto when they
came...
                    (MAMÁ LUPE starts to cry.)

                              ANA
Mom? Are you okay? ...
                    (ANA hugs her.)
Do you feel pain?
                    (beat)
Are you just happy about those memories?
                    (moved by her crying)
Oh, mamita...te amamos, mami.

                              EVA
We love you, prima.

                    ARMANDO
Te queremos, abuelita.

                     LAURA
Vas a estar bien, abuelita. You'll be fine. We'll stick together.

          (MAMÁ LUPE starts babbling and looks
          at her family. With great effort, she
          finally says something.)

                   MAMÁ LUPE
G-racias.

          (ANA, EVA, and ARMANDO look at each
          other, moved by hearing this. They
          hug each other.)

                  (BLACKOUT)

                (END OF PLAY)

BUT, BABE
_____

A Play in One Act

by

Samara Siskind

Cast of Characters

Andy: Male, college boy. Hispanic. Well-spoken.
                         Tolerant. Just wants to chill.

Julia: Female, college girl. Andy's girlfriend.
                         Non-Hispanic. Resolute. Just wants to
                         make a good impression.

SCENE
Miami

TIME
Christmas Eve

SETTING: A front porch somewhere in Miami.

AT RISE: The front porch of a house. A door with a
                                  wreath, bench, some twinkle lights. We
                                  hear party sounds, lively Latin music
                                  playing in the distance. JULIA and ANDY
                                  enter, holding hands.

                    ANDY
We're here.

                    JULIA
This is it?

                    ANDY
Mi casa es su casa. Well, my parents' casa es su casa.

                    JULIA
So this is where you grew up? It's exactly how I pictured it. I
love it.

                    ANDY
It has its charms.

                    JULIA
          (checking watch)
Andy, we're so late. It's already ten.

                    ANDY
We're right on time. Cuban time. The party has just begun.

                    JULIA
I'm nervous.

                    ANDY
Don't worry. They're going to love you.

                    JULIA
I wish it was just your Mom and Dad. I'm great with parents.
Parents just like, adore me for some reason, but it's not just them
in there. This is like your whole big, familia.

                    ANDY
Better to meet them all at once. Get it over with.

                              JULIA
                 (twirls, showing off her dress)
How do I look?

                              ANDY
Estás hermosa. Seriously, you look gorgeous. And very festive.
                 (beat)
Okay, a few warnings. Don't be offended if you hear a lot of
shouting. We Cubans can be loud. It may sound like we're fighting
or arguing, but we're not. It's just our way.

                              JULIA
Got it.

                              ANDY
You're going to get a lot of kisses on the cheek. Just go with it.
Drink the cafecito if they offer.

                              JULIA
Kisses, check. Drink the cafecito, I assume that's coffee, check.
Anything else I need to know?

                              ANDY
Don't bring up politics. Oh, and look out for Tío Raul. He's a
flirt. Ready? The party is out back.

                              JULIA
                 (deep breath)
Okay, Let's do this.

                              ANDY
Merry Christmas Eve.

                              JULIA
Merry Christmas Eve.

                 (They share a sweet kiss and exit
                 off to the backyard, hand in hand. A
                 few seconds later, JULIA runs back
                 on. She's upset, maybe even a little
                 sick. One hand is cupped over her
                 mouth. After a beat, ANDY runs in
                 after her.)

                              ANDY
Hey, you okay? Why'd you run out?

                              JULIA
                    (walking around in circles)
Oh my gosh, oh my gosh, oh my gosh, roasting...burning...
turning...fire.

                              ANDY
Hey, hey. I can't understand you, just breathe.

                              JULIA
Pig, pig, big pig, being tortured.

                              ANDY
Wait. You mean, the lechón?

                              JULIA
Does lechón mean pig murder in English?

                              ANDY
It's roasted pork. It's a traditional meal for Noche Buena.

                              JULIA
No. No. No, no, no, no, no. There is nothing buena about this
noche. Didn't you tell your Mom I was vegetarian?

                              ANDY
She said they weren't having one this year. One of my uncles must
have brought it. I would've warned you. I'm sorry.

                              JULIA
This isn't going to work. I can't stay here. I can't just stand
there and watch that, smell that, eat that-

                              ANDY
Julia-

                              JULIA
                    (manically swiping on phone)
It's okay. No worries. You stay. I'll get an Uber back to the
hotel.

                              ANDY
Hey, no. C'mon. We just got here.

                              JULIA
Do you know what my favorite movie was as a kid, Andy? Do you?!
Babe. *Babe* was my favorite movie. The little pig trying to find his

                              JULIA (cont.)
purpose. It's the movie that made me want to become a vegetarian
in the first place. Now I cannot go back there and watch them burn
Babe for Christmas dinner on that, that seriously messed up torture
device!

                              ANDY
It's a spit.

                              JULIA
Well, I spit on their spit. It's barbaric.

                              ANDY
I'm actually surprised they're cooking it that way. Someone usually
brings La Caja China.

                              JULIA
What is that? Like Chinese water torture? For the pig?

                              ANDY
Uh, no. It's a big metal and wooden box they cook it in.

                              JULIA
Well, that sounds equally lovely—I can't believe this. I-I
should've just gone home or stayed at the dorm for winter break.

                              ANDY
What? We agreed we'd do Thanksgiving with your family in Georgia
and Christmas in Miami with mine.

                              JULIA
That was before!

                              ANDY
Before what?

                              JULIA
Before I realized I had to report you all to the ASPCA!

                              ANDY
Don't you think you're overreacting?

                              JULIA
I'm not overreacting! You're under-reacting! You have no feeling!

ANDY

¡Oye! Tengo mucho sentimiento! I have plenty of feeling!

JULIA

Don't yell at me!

ANDY

I'm not yelling! I told you, we're volume control challenged!
Another Cuban content warning, we have bad tempers when provoked!

JULIA

Well, so do Alpha Delta Pi girls!!

ANDY

What's the big deal?! You know I eat meat! It never bothered you
before!

JULIA

I never had to witness the animal you were about to eat staring at
me with an apple stuck in its mouth! I can't unsee that, Andy!

ANDY

What can I say? These are my roots! I told you, it's tradition!

JULIA

Tradition is no excuse to serve the flesh of a poor defenseless
animal, while humiliating it for all to see!

ANDY

I mean, like they don't have barbecue in Georgia?

JULIA

Not like that!
                (checks phone)
There's an UberX five minutes away.

ANDY
                (taking phone)
¿Estás loca? You're not taking an Uber. It's Christmas Eve!

JULIA

Hey! Give me my phone! Andy!
                (ANDY plays keep away as JULIA tries
                to get it back.)

                        JULIA (cont.)
            (She finally gives up and stomps over
              to the bench where she plops down.)
    Fine. I'll just wait out here until it's over.

                          ANDY
    Good luck with that. We party all night. I'll bring you a blanket.
                (ANDY storms off, and JULIA slumps
                down, covering her face with her
                hands. Before he can fully exit,
                ANDY stops. He regains his composure
                and slowly returns to the bench next
                to JULIA.)
    So...

                          JULIA
    Our first fight.

                          ANDY
    Second.
                (JULIA looks at him.)
    When you read all my ex-texts from Camila?

                          JULIA
    Oh. Yeah. That was bad.

                          ANDY
                (setting phone on her lap)
    ...so. Are we going to camp out here all night, or are we going to
    go back in there and face the pig in the room?

                          JULIA
    It's not funny. I'm not going back there. It's like a crime
    scene...from *Lord of the Flies*.

                          ANDY
    Julia, I'm tired. I've been driving all day. I just want to see my
    family, have a drink and relax. I haven't been home from college
    since last Christmas. Can't you just take one for the team?

                          JULIA
    You want me to just pretend I'm okay with it? Put aside all of my
    beliefs?

                          ANDY
    I'm asking you to compromise. Show a little...tolerance. You know,
    Thanksgiving with your folks wasn't a picnic either.

JULIA

What? Because of the tofurkey? Mom was just honoring my dietary requests.

ANDY

No. Because of your Dad. He thought I was Mexican. He asked if we had enchiladas and turkey tacos for Thanksgiving dinner. Didn't you tell them I was Cuban?

JULIA

He what? You never told me that.

ANDY

You were in the bathroom.

JULIA

Why didn't you say anything?

ANDY

I didn't want to ruin the holiday. It didn't matter.

JULIA

It does matter.

ANDY

What matters is that I love his daughter. It was his first time meeting me. It was awkward, but you know, I dealt with it. I corrected him, explained that not all Hispanics are Mexican, then he passed the sweet potato casserole, and we moved on.

JULIA

Tallapoosa doesn't have a big Latin population. Not that that's a good excuse. I'm sorry. I feel like a jerk now.

ANDY

Next time we go over there, it'll be easier. He'll learn more about me, my culture. He'll accept me.

JULIA

He already has. They both loved you, Andy.

ANDY

Well, now it's your turn. To accept me.

                              JULIA
I do accept you!

                              ANDY
<u>All</u> of me. <u>And</u> them. See, it's not just about roasting a pig in
there. There are four generations under that roof. It's about
everyone having a drink in their hands, dancing, laughing, sharing
stories about the old days. It's chaos, and it's comfort, and I
love it. Roasting this pork tonight is as much a part of Christmas
for us as Santa and stockings are for you. Our relatives back in
Cuba would dream of having a feast this grand, able to fill so many
bellies. So, yes, this pig is being sacrificed, but like Babe, that
pig has a purpose—to feed us and bring us all together.

                              JULIA
That was quite a monologue.

                              ANDY
I'm not on the competitive debate team for nothing.

                              JULIA
                    (head nuzzling ANDY's neck)
I made a scene. I'm so embarrassed. Everyone's going to be like,
who's that stupid gringa Andy brought home?

                              ANDY
No one even noticed us come in. I told you, we're loud. It has its
advantages.

                              JULIA
                    (collecting herself)
Okay. I'm going back in. Noche Buena, take two.

                              ANDY
That's my girl.

                              JULIA
I don't want to offend anyone. Will there be anything else I can
eat?

                              ANDY
Are you kidding? There's black beans and rice, salad, yucca,
plantains. If my cousin Katie is here, there might even be a
vegetarian picadillo somewhere. Don't even get me started on
dessert. You're covered.

                    JULIA
It all sounds delicious.

                    ANDY
I can set us up playing dominoes with your back against the spit so
you don't have to see it.

                    JULIA
I don't know how to play.

                    ANDY
I'll teach you. You can teach your Dad. We can teach your Dad.
          (JULIA smiles.)
You can also sit with all the tías in the living room, or we can
dance, or help my Mom in the kitchen with the sides-

                    JULIA
I'll be okay. I have my big girl pantalones on.

                    ANDY
Bragas.

                    JULIA
What?

                    ANDY
Panties. Bragas in Spanish.

                    JULIA
Ah, okay. I have my big girl bragas on.

                    ANDY
Are you ready?

                    JULIA
Yes...but, warning. If Camila is in there, I'm taking her down.

          (A festive Christmas song plays.)

                    ANDY
          (wrapping arms around her)
If we're still together, I'll campaign for a vegan lechón next
year.

                    JULIA
              (squeezing him tighter)
Oh Andy, I love you.

                    ANDY
That'll do, babe. That'll do.

              (BLACKOUT)

              (END OF PLAY)

WHERE VOICES LINGER
_____

A Play in One Act

by

Jeremy Rafal

Cast of Characters

Antonio Lugano: 70, Filipino man, committed for
                               almost 50 years, clings to memories of
                               loved ones.

Nurse Schmidt: A compassionate young nurse tasked
                               with evaluating Antonio's release.
                               Caught between her role as a caregiver
                               and the institution's bureaucracy.

                              SCENE
                        An evaluation room,
               Wilmington Asylum for the Chronically Insane

                               Time
                         January 8, 1968

SETTING: Evaluation room in a psychiatric
                            facility.

AT RISE: The stage is dark except for a spotlight
                            illuminating ANTONIO LUGANO, a Filipino
                            man in his 70s. He is standing alone,
                            reading a letter, his face a mixture of
                            longing and resolve.

                           ANTONIO
                    (to the audience)
December 16th, 1967. My dearest Grace. It's almost Christmas, and
all of New York is buried under snow. You know how I've always loved
the snow—oh, how it brings me right back to you. There's something
about the way it blankets the world, turning it soft and still.
Yesterday, I slipped outside—just for a little while—and built a
snow castle. I even made a snow angel! Of course, the nurse ushered
me back in before long. I can hear you laughing at me saying, "I'd
take Manila's warm sun over all this dreariness." You never did
see the charm of winter, did you? The warmth of the Philippines,
day in and day out, would dull anyone's spirit! You're the lucky
one, getting to experience all four seasons—each one with its own
splendor, like a fresh story told every few months. The maple tree
outside my window is thick with snow now, but it reminds me of
you just the same. Those mornings in Chicago, our walks in Jackson
Park. I'll never forget our plans, dreaming of university together,
reading every book we could get our hands on. You'd tell me about
Henry Longfellow, and I'd tell you of Dr. José Rizal—his travels,
his books, and the Filipino spirit he carried to distant places. I
read everything he wrote, every last word. And you would read them
all with me.

                    (Lights up on an evaluation room at
                    the Wilmington Asylum for the Chronic
                    Insane.)At the center, a table with
                    a pile of folders and papers. NURSE
                    SCHMIDT sits on one side. She takes
                    notes as she listens.)

                           NURSE SCHMIDT
Mr. Lugano?

                           ANTONIO
                    (sitting opposite NURSE SCHMIDT)
And you'd tell me about your grandmother and how you used to sneak
into her kitchen to steal a piece of her apple pie cooling on the
windowsill. And I'd laugh and tell you about my cousin Arnel in the

                         ANTONIO (cont.)
Philippines—

                         NURSE SCHMIDT
Would you like me to take your letter? I can put it the mail.
               (ANTONIO doesn't answer.)
Mr. Lugano?

                         ANTONIO
It's Antonio, Nurse Schmidt. That old witch Nurse Jones used to
call me Mr. Lugano. You're much nicer than she was.

                         NURSE SCHMIDT
Your letter is beautiful, Mr...I mean Antonio. Would you like me
to mail it?

                         ANTONIO
I would like to keep this one, Nurse.

               (NURSE SCHMIDT opens a folder from
               the pile, revealing a few letters
               and a single photograph. She gently
               extends her hand, offering to take
               his letter once more.)

                         NURSE SCHMIDT
Are you sure? It's been a few weeks since you wrote it.

                         ANTONIO
We both know where those letters end up.

                         NURSE SCHMIDT
I will try to make sure these letters will—

                         ANTONIO
Wait. That photo...is that...where did you...

                         NURSE SCHMIDT
This? Oh...I...can't...
               (quickly closing folder)
We have to hold on to this one.

                         ANTONIO
Of course you do. I may be in an asylum, but I'm not blind to what's
going on. You're just going to shove them in some attic and forget
about them.

NURSE SCHMIDT

I'm sorry, Antonio. I've been trying to get your letters. Wait, is that what Nurse Jones told you?

ANTONIO

Her? Hah. She'd be the last person to tell me anything about this place.

NURSE SCHMIDT

Why do you say that?

ANTONIO

That woman! She never had a lick of respect for any of us. Treated us all like dirt.

NURSE SCHMIDT

I heard you were actually one of her favorite patients. She liked it when you played the piano.

ANTONIO

She sure didn't show it. But I figured it out early—just play her little games, stay polite, keep your head down. Don't give her a reason to come after you. The others, they couldn't manage that, so she treated them like crap all the time!

NURSE SCHMIDT

I'm sure she was just trying to do her job.

ANTONIO

That's what Dr. Markus always said when he first came on board here. Always sticking up for her, you know? She'd been here the longest. What could he do? Just had to wait her out, bide his time until she finally...retired.
          (shouting at no one in particular)
Good riddance, you hear me? I outlasted you, old witch!

NURSE SCHMIDT
          (looking around)
Are you talking to Nurse Jones, Antonio?

ANTONIO

You know, Nurse Schmidt, for the six months I've known you now, you're alright.

                         NURSE SCHMIDT
Thank you. That is very kind for you to say.
                    (beat)
You have such a sweet and special way of talking to Grace,
Antonio. Would you tell me more about her? How was—what did she—

                         ANTONIO
You're different from the others.

                         NURSE SCHMIDT
What was she like...I mean, do you still hear her voice?

                         ANTONIO
It wasn't her fault, you know. Her parents.

                         NURSE SCHMIDT
Her parents? You mean Grace's parents?

                         ANTONIO
What we had. They just didn't understand. That's why I forgive them
for what they did.
                    (beat)
Tell me, Nurse Schmidt. Have you ever been in love?

                         NURSE SCHMIDT
Well, I—I'm just trying to write a report here, Mr. Lugano. I...

                         ANTONIO
You've got a good heart, Nurse Schmidt. I can tell. I just pray
you'll never find out what it's like for it to be broken.

                         NURSE SCHMIDT
                    (hesitating)
Well...my Carl just proposed right at midnight on New Year's Eve.
Timed it perfectly with the countdown!

                         ANTONIO
Congratulations, Nurse Schmidt! I bet your folks must be over the
moon for you.
                         NURSE SCHMIDT
My parents were certainly shocked when they first met my Carl. I was
convinced they'd disown me right then and there.

                         ANTONIO
Why would they?

NURSE SCHMIDT

Carl isn't exactly...white.

ANTONIO

Oh?

NURSE SCHMIDT

We were honestly terrified our parents wouldn't be open-minded, you know? But Carl and I, we're in love, and we weren't going to let anything stand in our way. Turns out, they were mostly worried for us—how society might treat us. But then Loving vs. Virginia happened. You must've heard about it, right?

ANTONIO

Seems you forget, Nurse. We don't have the same access to news in here that you do.

NURSE SCHMIDT

Just last summer, the Supreme Court ruled that states couldn't ban interracial marriage. We were on cloud nine when we heard the news! Right then, I knew that Carl was going to propose. I just didn't know when. When he did, it was such a wonderful surprise!

                    (The news visibly affects ANTONIO.
                    He takes it in and holds in his
                    happiness.)

ANTONIO

Well, that's fantastic news! That boy better make sure he takes great care of you!

NURSE SCHMIDT
                    (smiling, taking the advice)
Carl is the sweetest man I know and he certainly will...I just wish my grandmother...
                    (beat)
Well, we should keep going, shall we? Do you still hear voices?

ANTONIO

Most of them have stopped. Once in a while, I'll hear someone.

NURSE SCHMIDT

Who do you hear?

                    ANTONIO
I'll tell you who I don't hear anymore. Edwin and Enrique.

                  NURSE SCHMIDT
Edwin and Enrique?

                    ANTONIO
Yes, they're the worst. They're the ones who kept yapping in my
head to do horrible things.

                  NURSE SCHMIDT
                 (looking at the chart)
Horrible things? Like the incident here...Zofia?

                    ANTONIO
Zofia. The Polish lady? I...

                  NURSE SCHMIDT
It says here Zofia was...looks like this was twenty years back,
sometime in the 40s. Looks like she also loved your piano playing.

                    ANTONIO
Yes, I played Chopin for her.

                  NURSE SCHMIDT
I'd love to hear you play sometime.

                    ANTONIO
Too bad they took the piano away...what did they say again?
Because it was 'hazardous' to the patients. What a shame. Maybe Dr.
Markus can bring back the piano. What do you think?

                  NURSE SCHMIDT
I can bring it up the next time I see him.

                    ANTONIO
Good.

                  NURSE SCHMIDT
                 (looking at her files)
It says here, Zofia was...pushed. Could you tell me what happened
that day?

                    ANTONIO
Zofia was a sweet lady. Polish. Loved Chopin. We got along just fine,

ANTONIO (cont.)

most days. But then one day, she saw me planning an escape and
something, something snapped in her. She had one of her episodes,
started calling me—calling me,well, a 'dirty little oriental.' She
wouldn't stop. Just kept yelling and yelling. Stop it!
> (ANTONIO abruptly stands, shouting
> at no one in particular.)

Stop. Stop! This is all your fault, you scoundrels. Get out. <u>Get
out of my head</u>! Leave me alone!

NURSE SCHMIDT
> (reaches out to ANTONIO)

Hey, hey. Antonio. Antonio! I'm here! I'm right here!

ANTONIO
> (calming down)

Grace? Grace, is that you? Where are you?

NURSE SCHMIDT

No, Mr. Lugano. It's me. Nurse Schmidt. You're okay. You're
here. Here, sit.

ANTONIO

Grace? What? Nurse Schmidt...

NURSE SCHMIDT

You had a little episode, but it looks like you were able to handle
it. Let me get you some water.
> (ANTONIO settles down as she brings
> him some water.)

Drink up. You're doing great...we should continue this tomorrow.

ANTONIO

No, I am fine. I just need a moment. Zofia...was my friend.

NURSE SCHMIDT

Are you sure we can go on?

ANTONIO

Let's just keep on going. It'll be fine. Well, I...I tried to ignore
them, believe me, but Edwin and Enrique wouldn't have any of that.
It was like they took over and they made me shove her into the
bushes. I couldn't stop them...and... Anyway, the rest should be
in the chart, shouldn't it?

                    NURSE SCHMIDT
                (looking through the files)
It says here no major injuries after the incident. Minor scratches
on her calves and shoulders.

                    ANTONIO
Except she passed weeks after that day.

                    NURSE SCHMIDT
Well, I...you shouldn't feel guilty about her passing. It was weeks
after the incident.

                    ANTONIO
Like I said. You're different from the other nurses.

                    NURSE SCHMIDT
You say that these two voices—

                    ANTONIO
Edwin and Enrique.

                    NURSE SCHMIDT
How often do they speak to you?

                    ANTONIO
Oh, not much anymore, except it don't look like it after
today, huh?

                    NURSE SCHMIDT
Sometimes certain things could trigger these voices unexpectedly.
But you were able to come back from it on your own just now. What
about the other voices?

                    ANTONIO
Most of them are gone. Sometimes Maria comes back, but she's
harmless. She likes to tell her jokes.

                    NURSE SCHMIDT
Even...Grace?
                (ANTONIO doesn't answer.)
Antonio? Mr. Lugano?

                    ANTONIO
I don't want her to go.

NURSE SCHMIDT
Is that why you still write letters to her?

ANTONIO
It keeps her close to me.

NURSE SCHMIDT
When...when was the last time you spoke to Grace, Antonio?

ANTONIO
            (smiling)
You know, Nurse. You remind me of Grace. Just a little.

NURSE SCHMIDT
Mr. Lugano. Antonio. When was the last time you saw Grace?

ANTONIO
That should also be in my file, shouldn't it?

NURSE SCHMIDT
Yes, that is true, but I would like to hear it from you.

ANTONIO
A couple months after I came to Wilmington.

NURSE SCHMIDT
And when did you come to Wilmington?

ANTONIO
It was 1919. When her parents threw me in this looney bin. I
shouldn't have broken into their house, I know that, but what was
I supposed to do? I just wanted to see her. They didn't approve of
me, not one bit. They'd stare at me—at the color of my skin, like I
was some animal beneath them! And Grace, she couldn't do anything.
How could she? I—I... But I'm hopeful she'd still visit...she could
walk in and...I'd like to finish reading the letter now.

NURSE SCHMIDT
It's a beautiful letter, Antonio. But you've read it five times
today already...Grace would be...

ANTONIO
Nurse Schmidt. May I ask you a question?

NURSE SCHMIDT
Well, I...sure. You may ask me a question.

                    ANTONIO
Tell me, why are we talking again? Why is it that, all of a sudden,
you're meeting with us more in the last few weeks than you have in
the last forty years?

                  NURSE SCHMIDT
Well, Antonio. I've been assigned to help Dr. Markus evaluate you.
You have been here for a very long time and we want to make a
recommendation to discharge you.

                    ANTONIO
Discharge?

                  NURSE SCHMIDT
When Dr. Markus took over, he thought it was time to reevaluate
this place. He believes you may have been kept here longer than you
should've been.

                    ANTONIO
But what if Grace comes to visit? How will she find me?

                  NURSE SCHMIDT
Mr Luga...Antonio. Grace is—looking over your files, it seems your
case wasn't all that severe. With the advances we've made in mental
health treatment, there are ways to help you manage the voices
without needing to stay confined here at Wilmington.

                    ANTONIO
Grace. I need to be here just in case she—

                  NURSE SCHMIDT
We believe your condition may have been triggered by a traumatic
event, which led to a deep state of depression. That depression
likely caused you to hear voices for a time, but according to your
records, your case wasn't severe. It's nothing that can't be
managed with counseling. Our recommendation is for you to return to
your family and seek counseling support as needed.

                    ANTONIO
You want me to leave?

                  NURSE SCHMIDT
You are free to go, Mr. Lugano.

                    ANTONIO
Free?

NURSE SCHMIDT

It says here you've filed for a request to be discharged multiple times, and you've tried to escape multiple times.

ANTONIO

It's too late, Nurse. Fifty years in these walls! Where am I to go? My friends? Gone, long forgotten.
            (pausing, searching for her face)
And now, you're...telling me to leave?

NURSE SCHMIDT

I'm afraid we will have to transfer you a home then, Mr. Lugano.

ANTONIO

No! I will not leave. I've been locked up here for fifty years- fifty years! And now, you're just tossing me out onto the streets? Tell me, what am I supposed to do? How do you expect an old man to survive in a foreign place and time?

NURSE SCHMIDT

Please calm down, Mr. Lugano. There's a chance the hospital may be closing down so we may have no choice but to find you a home.

ANTONIO

So that's what this is all about? After all these years, you can't even keep this place going? And now you're just looking for somewhere to dump us? My soul is tied to these walls. Pushing me out there——it's no better than taking away my freedom all those years ago.

NURSE SCHMIDT

I...you're right, Antonio. This place...it's certainly not perfect, but it's been your home. And for me, it's been a connection to my grandmother. I wish I could promise everything will be okay...Can I give you something?
            (She hands him a photograph.)
I am probably breaking all sorts of protocol here, but when my family and I were going through my grandmother's things last summer, I found this.
            (ANTONIO looks at the photograph and
            has a moment of recognition.
It took me a while to put the pieces together, but when I saw some of the old photographs from your file...and then found this picture, I couldn't believe it. I tried to ask my Grandma Grace about them, but her Alzheimer's had taken too much. Still, when she saw the photo, she said two words——'Chicago'and your name. 'Antonio.'

ANTONIO

That dress...I remember that day at Jackson Park. Like a Monet painting. We talked about Rizal and Longfellow and… Where is she now? Is she still...

NURSE SCHMIDT

A couple weeks before Christmas, she...passed. I wanted so much to tell you, Mr. Lugano. But, well...my job wouldn't allow it. I could get fired for saying this now. But, since this place might close down anyway, it might not matter anymore. Before she passed, I took some of your letters and read them to her. Every time I did, she wouldn't say a word, but I swear, I'd see the slightest spark in her face.

ANTONIO

She...she remembered me. After all these years.
            (pause, then a soft smile)
You know, Nurse. You remind me of Grace. Just a little.
            (beat)
I'd like to finish reading my letter now.
            (NURSE SCHMIDT nods. Lights down.
            Spotlight on ANTONIO as he continues
            to read the letter.)
...how you used to sneak into her kitchen to steal a piece of her apple pie cooling on the windowsill. And I'd laugh and tell you about my cousin Arnel in the Philippines—how we'd play in the rain like a couple of fools, even though our parents didn't approve. We'd come back covered in mud, but oh, was it worth it!
            (folds the letter gently, holds it
            close to his heart, and looks out in
            the distance)
Oh, Grace. Next time we see each other, do teach me how to make your grandma's famous apple pie. I've waited so long. And maybe we'll walk again in Jackson Park, like we always planned, in a world that doesn't keep us apart...

            (Lights fade out.)

            (BLACKOUT)

            (END OF PLAY)

A WALK IN THE NIGHT

_____

A Play in One Act

by

Paul Bowman

<u>Cast of Characters</u>

Angela: Female, 50 to 60's

Juan: Male, 20s

Maria: Female, 20s or younger

<u>SCENE</u>
A living room

<u>TIME</u>
Christmas Eve, Present day

ACT I

SCENE 1

SETTING: A house in farm country.

AT RISE: ANGELA's living room. A well decorated
                                space with drinks, cookies and ornamental
                                candles set about. At the front of the
                                stage is a blanketed rocking chair. Near
                                it, wrapped presents. A garbage can sits
                                near the chair as ANGELA paces around on
                                the phone.

                                ANGELA
Come on. Answer.
                        (The phone rings repeatedly. She
                        hangs up. She dials another number
                        and waits.)
James. You promised to stop by. Where are you? Something happen?
Give me a call.
                        (She dials another number.)
Mary. The dinner's tonight. Have you forgotten? Call me.
                        (ANGELA paces. She picks up a present
                        then puts it back and dials another
                        number.)
Josephine! When...what...you're kidding me...oh, I see. Well, I
guess it couldn't be helped...I understand. I understand—no, I'm
not mad. A little disappointed. I went to all this trouble, and no
one's bothering to show up. When can you come? I see. Well, tell
the children I made them my special chocolate brownies, and I won't
eat a one. I promise.
                        (laughs)
Okay. Have a good Christmas. I will. Merry Christmas. Bye.
                        (ANGELA hangs up and stares at the
                        garbage can. She eyes the presents,
                        picking up one and placing it in the
                        garbage can. She chooses another
                        gift, tossing it in the can. She
                        does this until all the gifts are in
                        the garbage. She ties up the bag and
                        reclines in the chair. The lights dim
                        as ANGELA closes her eyes until the
                        abrupt sound of knocking on the door.
                        ANGELA awakes and stands.)
Who's there?

                         ANGELA (cont.)
               (continued knocking)
     Hello?

                    (ANGELA opens the door, and an
                    exhausted man stumbles into her home
                    and falls on the floor.)

                         JUAN
     Ayúdame! Ayúdame!

                         ANGELA
               (retreating)
     Eww.

                         JUAN
               (shivering)
     Agua.

                         ANGELA
     Get out. Get out of my house!
                    (ANGELA backs to the right side of
                    the stage, grabbing one of the tall
                    ornamental candle holders, holding
                    it like it's a bat. She stands over
                    JUAN, ready to swing. But JUAN lays
                    unmoving. Unresponsive. She walks
                    around him, watching. She grabs her
                    phone, but JUAN jumps up, scaring
                    her.)

                         JUAN
     Agua. Agua.

                    (JUAN gestures to her table, imitating
                    bringing a glass to his lips.)

                         ANGELA
     You want water?

                         JUAN
               (nodding)
     Agua.

                         ANGELA
     Who are you? Where did you come from?

                         JUAN
     Agua. Por favor.

ANGELA

Speak English.

JUAN

Agua.

ANGELA
                    (ANGELA grabs one of the glasses of
                    water from the table, still clutching
                    the candlestick holder as she
                    approaches.)
Don't you try anything.
                    (She gives him the glass.)
Where did you come from?

JUAN

Gracias. Gracias.

          (JUAN drinks some more.)

ANGELA

Don't you have a coat? It's cold out there. I'm calling for help!

          (She places the candlestick holder
          on the floor and grabs her phone. JUAN
          shakes his head, walking towards her.

JUAN

No.

ANGELA

Sorry. This is the way it's gotta be, buddy. Only you're not my
buddy.
                    (JUAN frantically gestures to the
                    door.)
What?!
                    (JUAN grabs her hand, pulling her to
                    the door.)
No, I'm not leaving. With you? No.
                    (JUAN continues to pull her and the
                    two struggle before ANGELA rips her
                    hand away.)
Now, I'm really calling the police.
                    (JUAN holds up his hands in surrender
                    and points to the water glass.)
Another one? After all this...fine.

ANGELA (cont.)
(ANGELA grabs another water glass
from the table. He shakes his head
and motions like he's twisting off a
cap on a bottle.)
Stay here. Don't touch anything.
(She exits the stage and returns with
a bottle. He accepts it gratefully.)
Okay. Leave now.
(She points to the door. JUAN shakes
his head.)
I'm not calling the authorities on you, okay? Just go.
(JUAN begins pacing around the room.
ANGELA chases after him.)
Excuse me! This is my house! You can't come barging in—
(JUAN grabs a blanket from the chair
and wraps it around him.)
You want a blanket? Fine. Take it. What is it with your types
anyway? You want everything...Just take it!
(JUAN nods his head several times
in thanks. ANGELA waits for him to
leave, but JUAN again gestures that
she should leave with him.)
What? No. I'm not leaving with you.
(JUAN points to the phone in her
pocket.)
I said no! Leave!
(ANGELA shoos him out of her house.
Moments later, her phone dings.)
Severe weather alert? Snowy roads. Shelter in place?
(looking at the ceiling)
God, are you telling me to do this, or am I just a stupid fool?
(She waits for a moment then pockets
her phone and runs off stage. She re-
enters with a flashlight while putting
on a winter coat. She shouts off-
stage in the opposite direction.)
Hey! Wait!

(ANGELA exits stage right.)

(BLACKOUT)

(END OF SCENE)

ACT I

SCENE 2

SETTING: A cold night.

AT RISE: JUAN and ANGELA enter. JUAN, in the lead
                            shines the flashlight on the floor. They go
                            slowly. Sounds of the night wind.

                    JUAN
Gracias. Gracias.

                    ANGELA
How much further?
                    (JUAN gestures to continue as they
                walk back and forth across the stage.)
You know, we really shouldn't even be out here. I really shouldn't
even be out here! I don't even know you, or trust you.
                    (ANGELA turns to leave, but JUAN grabs
                her arm and points straight ahead.)
Fine. Alright.
                    (speaking to self)
I'm just tired of trusting people. I do everything, and they just
put me aside. Can't make it to Christmas Eve Dinner, but if one of
them needs a loan it's "Aunt Angela could I borrow two hundred?
I'll pay you back I promise." Except they conveniently forget to.

                    (JUAN goes forward then stops.
                ANGELA stops.)

                    JUAN
Aquí.

                    ANGELA
So, no English then?

                    (The flashlight beam dims as they near
                    the center stage. A young woman,
                    MARIA, lies on the ground. She wears a
                    flimsy jacket. Tucked under the jacket
                    cradled to her chest is a baby. JUAN
                    runs to her and falls beside her.)

                              MARIA
                        (waking up and weary)
          Juan. Juan!

                    (JUAN unscrews the cap from a water
                    bottle and gives it to her. She
                    drinks. ANGELA approaches. JUAN looks
                    at ANGELA and points to the bottle.)

                              JUAN
                        (to ANGELA)
          Agua.

                              ANGELA
          What in the world?

                    (JUAN gives the flashlight to ANGELA.
                    She shines it on MARIA as he puts the
                    blanket around her. He strokes her
                    cheek and turns to ANGELA.)

                              JUAN
          Maria.

                              ANGELA
          You didn't tell me she was out here! In the cold! By herself! Why
          didn't you tell me? You couldn't, but you were trying to. I wasn't
          listening.
                              (JUAN gently peels back the blanket
                              and MARIA'S jacket to look at the
                              baby. He touches its head. The
                              flashlight beam shines on the baby.
                              ANGELA gasps.)
          A baby?! She has a baby?! What?
                              (ANGELA falls to the floor beside
                              MARIA. She leans in to look at the
                              infant.)
          So small. Was it just born? Out here?
                              (ANGELA is near tears.)
          I didn't believe...I should have trusted. I'm sorry.
                              (JUAN mimes talking on the phone.
                              ANGELA takes out hers and calls.)

ANGELA (cont.)

Nine-one-one. I have an emergency. I need an ambulance. Ambulance. I said ambulance. This woman needs to be taken to a hospital. She and her baby...I don't know how they survived. It's a miracle...You go down State Road 66 until you get to Bethel Lane. You'll see the two silos. Just past that is a gravel road...Hello? Silos. Gravel road. You'll see my flashlight. Please hurry.

JUAN

Gracias. Gracias.

        (ANGELA stands and stares down at
        the child.)

MARIA

Gracias.

ANGELA

Beautiful baby...Oh.
        (ANGELA reaches into her coat pocket
        and retrieves a sandwich bag that
        contains two brownies.)
I made them for my relatives, but...You must be hungry.
        (ANGELA gives MARIA and JUAN
        brownies. They eat.)
Well, somebody likes my brownies. Good...Here.
        (JUAN finishes his brownie. ANGELA
        removes her coat and gives it to
        JUAN. ANGELA'S blouse is long-sleeved
        and white. A shiny, silky white. JUAN
        stares quizzically.)
Keep it. I'll be okay. I'm an old country gal. Used to get up at five thirty to feed the hogs.
        (JUAN drapes the coat over MARIA.)

JUAN

Tú eres...angel.

ANGELA

No. Angela. My name is Angela.

JUAN

Angel.

                          ANGELA
You're not saying it right. Angela.

                           JUAN
                 (points to the night sky)
Angel. Angel.

                          ANGELA
                 (moved by the compliment)
Angel.

                 (Lights dim as the flashlight beam
                 down on MARIA and her baby. The sound
                 of sirens offstage.)

                      (BLACKOUT)

                      (END OF PLAY)

CHRISTMAS CACTUS

_____

A Play in One Act

by

Emma Denson

Cast of Characters

Jada: Female, 14, black. Born and raised
                         in small-town Alabama with an accent to
                         match. Curious, bubbly, and feisty. She
                         is the sunshine to Moss' cloudy skies.
                         Despite her cheerfulness, she hides some
                         sadness of her own.

Moss: Male, 78, Irish American with a County
                         Cork, Irish accent. Moved to Alabama from
                         New York City 40 years ago. Despite his
                         grumpy exterior, he has a soft side that
                         can be coaxed out by the right people.

SCENE
A small, unknown town in Alabama

TIME
Present day

```
SETTING:                    A Victorian style home.

AT RISE:                    Lights up on a study in a Victorian home.
                            From off stage, we hear a contemporary
                            cover of a classic Christmas song, along
                            with the murmur of southern American
                            voices. The door to the study opens, and
                            JADA enters. She closes it quietly behind
                            her and lets out a breath, relieved to
                            have escaped the adults. She looks at her
                            surroundings: a bookshelf (immaculate),
                            a desk (no clutter), and a rocking chair
                            (with a neatly folded quilt draped over
                            it). JADA hesitantly grabs a book off the
                            shelf, sinking into the rocking chair.
                            She rocks back and forth, reading, when
                            the door opens behind her. MOSS enters.
```

                          MOSS
This room isn't part of the open house.

                          JADA
               (jumping from the rocker)
Sorry. I was jist-

                          MOSS
If you're after stealin' from me, I'd advise you ta—

                          JADA
I'm not <u>stealin'</u> nothin'. Jist bored, s'all. Momma's been down
there talkin' to Mrs. Bryant about our homeroom's Christmas party
for ages, and I wanna see the other houses 'fore it gets too late.

                          MOSS
They'll be closed by now.

                          JADA
What? What time is it?

                          MOSS
Nine.

                          JADA
Already? But we ain't even been down Birch Street yet.

                              MOSS
                    (distracted, checking room)
That's a shame.

                              JADA
There's this one down there that's all the way from 1880. You seen
it?

                              MOSS
Uh-huh.

                              JADA
It's the oldest one in the whole historic district, and there's
this chandelier that, when the candlelight hits it jist right, it
looks like a galaxy in there. Like a billion stars exploded all
over that old lady's ceiling.

                              MOSS
Sounds nice.

                              JADA
How old's your house?

                              MOSS
Didn't you read the sign out front?

                              JADA
I did, but usually folks like when I ask. Gives 'em a chance to
talk about when the house was built, what great shape the original
floors are in, all that.

                              MOSS
I don't like ta be asked.

                              JADA
Have you been hidin' this whole time? I don't remember seein' you
downstairs. Jist that girl with the curly hair, and the funny name—

                              MOSS
Her name is Roisin, and it's not a funny—

                              JADA
Sorry. I shouldn't have said—

                          MOSS
I told her mam we should have named her "Rose." It'll be easier to
say, but she insisted we had to honor my—

                          JADA
She's your daughter?

                          MOSS
Wha?

                          JADA
Roisin! She's your daughter?

                          MOSS
Well, yes—

                          JADA
I can see it now that I'm lookin' close. Got the same nose.

                          MOSS
Don't look at me nose.

                          JADA
Why not? It ain't bad.

                          MOSS
What's that supposed ta mean?

                          JADA
Jist that as far as noses go, I seen worse.

                          MOSS
Won't yer mam be looking for ye?

                          JADA
                    (ignoring question)
If you don't like talkin' about your home, why open it every year?

                          MOSS
Wha?

                          JADA
Why do all this if it ain't fun for you?

                         MOSS
Going to the dentist isn't exactly fun, but we all gotta do things
we don't like much.

                         JADA
Yeah, but that's health-wise. This is optional, right? There're
other houses on this street that ain't open.

                         MOSS
Just something I do.

                         JADA
But you ain't <u>have</u> to.

                         MOSS
If yis must know, young lady, my wife started it. Years ago.

                         JADA
So she's the one who likes to host?

                         MOSS
Yes.

                         JADA
              (picking up desk portrait)
This her?

                         MOSS
              (patting a decorative urn)
Yes...this is her too.

                         JADA
              (staring at him briefly then setting
              down the picture frame quickly and
              gently.)
Oh-
              (bowing to urn)
Nice to meet you. You got a lovely home.

                         MOSS
              (hiding small smile)
Don't get cheeky with me.

                         JADA
What else am I s'posed to do when you introduce me to your <u>dead</u> <u>wife</u>?

                        MOSS
I don't know.

                        JADA
Exactly.

                        MOSS
You could try "I'm sorry for your loss."

                        JADA
Do you <u>like</u> the pityin' looks?

                        MOSS
No.

                        JADA
The "I'm so sorrys." The "what can I dos?"

                        MOSS
No!

                        JADA
That's what I thought. But a little joke never killed nobody.
              (turning to urn)
Unless—

                        MOSS
Stop.

                        JADA
Is that why you don't smile no more? You afraid...
              (whispering)
...it'll happen again?

          (JADA laughs. MOSS doesn't.)

                        MOSS
Didn't your parents ever teach you to respect your elders?

                        JADA
My daddy always said, "Laughter is the best medicine." But he never
met as hard a case as you, so jury's still out.

                                    MOSS
What do you know about grief anyway, huh?

                                    JADA
'Scuse me?

                                    MOSS
You're what? Twelve?

                                    JADA
Fourteen.

                                    MOSS
Fourteen. A <u>child</u>. What on earth could you know about what it means
to lose someone?

                                    JADA
You don't know nothin' 'bout me. 'Bout my life.

                                    MOSS
I know you like to make morbid jokes about Helene.

                                    JADA
Who?

                                    MOSS
My <u>wife</u>.

                                    JADA
Right.

                                    MOSS
And I know you're obsessed with these ridiculous Christmas open
houses, but it's a stupid tradition—

                                    JADA
It ain't stupid—

                                    MOSS
And you're right! I don't have to do them. I've put up with strangers
coming into my home, looking at my China cabinet, twisting the
original brass knobs, for years. Well, thank you for reminding me.
I don't have to do this. Some traditions are meant to be broken.

JADA

You know, for an old man, you don't know much of nothin'.

MOSS

Now, young lady. I've had about-

JADA

But hey, don't stop opening your home 'cause of me. Believe me, I ain't coming back.

MOSS

Great!

JADA

Fine!

MOSS

Get!

JADA

I'm goin'!

(JADA grabs the knob, pausing.)

MOSS

I said-

JADA

C.S. Lewis.

MOSS

...what?

JADA

He's got some good stuff on it—grief. I recommend startin' with *Problem of Pain*...well, anyway. Merry Christmas.

(JADA turns the knob.)

MOSS

Wait.
(JADA stops.)
Who was it? The person you lost—who was it?

                         JADA
                   (closing the door)
My sister.

                         MOSS
Oh, that's—that's horrible.

                         JADA
Yeah.

                         MOSS
How old?

                         JADA
Seven.

                         MOSS
Jesus...cancer?

                         JADA
Don't want to talk about it.

                         MOSS
Helene had pancreatic.

                         JADA
One of the worst ones, ain't it?

                         MOSS
Yes.

                         JADA
Thought so. I'm sorry.

                         MOSS
Thank you. Me too...so...I know how you—

                         JADA
No, you don't.

                         MOSS
But, I thought—

                         JADA
I never said "yes."

                    MOSS
Right. Of course.

                    JADA
          (silent for a moment)
...she loved Christmas.

                    MOSS
Did she now?

                    JADA
Mhm. When we did these tours, she'd sneak way too many cookies in
her pockets. I pretended I ain't see, but now and then one of them
hosts would catch her, but she was so cute, even when she got caught
she got away with it.

                    MOSS
Did she like caroling?

                    JADA
Yeah.

                    MOSS
Was she any good?

                    JADA
Couldn't carry a tune in a bucket!

                    MOSS
Helene couldn't either! But God, I'd give anything to hear her
screech out "Joy to the World" one more time.

                    JADA
          (silent for a moment)
You know I ain't like this time of year for a while either. Made me
sad. And angry.

                    MOSS
What changed?

                    JADA
I saw it was killin' my folks. Me sittin' quiet on Christmas
mornin', not touchin' Momma's special pecan pancakes, or starin'
out the window instead of talkin' to 'em. It was like they lost two
daughters that day instead of one. One day, I jist got fed up with
bein' sad. Maia wouldn't want that. That was her name——Maia. Ain't
it pretty?

                                    MOSS
Very pretty.

                                    JADA
I finally went to her side of the room and started goin' through
some of her old things. I found her Looney Toons DVD set. Put it
on, and for the first time in a long time, I—I laughed. And then I
couldn't stop. Finally my dad came by and watched it with me, and
<u>he</u> laughed. We laughed 'til we cried. Good tears this time.

                                    MOSS
"Laughter is the best medicine."

                                    JADA
Yep. Eventually, I could go to school again without having as many
panic attacks, and I could say her name without crying. Though I
still hate the sound of fireworks or loud trucks. Sometimes even
popcorn.
                    (MOSS looks tenderly at JADA,
                     putting two and two together.)
Shame too. Popcorn used to be one of my favorites.

                                    MOSS
That man they arrested a few years ago—who broke into Elmwood Park
Elementary.

                                    JADA
You remember it?

                                    MOSS
Course I do. It was awful.

                                    JADA
Yeah.

                                    MOSS
So Maia was one of the kids who...
                    (JADA nods.)
I'm so sorry. I'm so very, very sorry.

                                    JADA
Thought we agreed we both hate being pitied.

                                    MOSS
Right. Of course. Well, I think your Maia and my Helene would've
liked each other very, very much.

                         JADA
I think so too.

                         MOSS
You know, I know your sister's name, but I don't think I ever
caught yours.

                         JADA
                 (with an extended hand)
Jada.

                         MOSS
                 (shaking it)
Moss.

                         JADA
Moss? Like that green stuff that grows on rocks?

                         MOSS
Short for "Morris." It's Irish.

                         JADA
Are you Irish?

                         MOSS
Irish-American. My mam and da came over from Cork before I was
born.

                         JADA
That's cool. Maybe I'll go there one day. Ireland.

                         MOSS
You'd like it.

                         JADA
Think you'll ever go back?

                         MOSS
I dunno. I'm kind of old, y'know?

                         JADA
Coulda fooled me.

                         MOSS
                 (with a small laugh)
Yeah, well. Maybe, kid, maybe.

                        JADA
...Can I give Helene something?

                        MOSS
Um, sure. I guess.
                    (JADA takes off her necklace and
                    drapes it around the urn.)
What is that?

                        JADA
It was Maia's.

                        MOSS
Jada. You can't give me this.

                        JADA
It's not for you. It's for Helene. Besides, I'll come back to see
it.

                        MOSS
You will?

                        JADA
S'long as you have an open house again next year...

                        MOSS
Oh, you're a cheeky one, aren't you?

                        JADA
That a yes?
                    (They exchange small smiles. MOSS
                    nods. JADA hugs him, catching him by
                    surprise. He hugs her back.)
Bye, Moss. Merry Christmas.

                        MOSS
                    (smiling)
The plaque outside says this house was built in 1914, but some
local historians have disputed that, saying it might have been as
much as four years earlier, in 1910.

                        JADA
                    (stopping and turning back)
Oh, really?

(She smiles, and he walks towards her.
They walk towards the exit together.)

MOSS

Yes. Now, what's really great about this house is the floors. All
original cherry.

JADA

Is it called cherry because it's kinda red?

MOSS

Sure is. Now, I don't normally let people into the breakfast room,
but we do have a chandelier in there—

JADA

A chandelier?

MOSS

Word on the street is you're a fan of those. Something about it
looking like a "galaxy."

(Their voices fade. The lights dim,
except for a spot that focuses on
the urn and necklace. An underscoring
of Christmas music plays as the spot
fades to black.)

(BLACK OUT)

(END OF PLAY)

MEET THE PLAYWRIGHTS

Russell Nichols is an African American playwright and speculative fiction writer whose work blends social consciousness with a lyrical command of language. Raised in Richmond, California, he began as a journalist before giving up his possessions in 2011 to travel the world with his wife, a nomadic journey that continues to shape his art. His global perspective fuels stories that probe identity, injustice, and the imaginative futures of marginalized communities. An "endangered journalist" turned boundary-pushing storyteller, Nichols creates plays and fiction that challenge and illuminate. More of his work can be found at russellnichols.com.

Rohan Magerman is a South African playwright and writer from Cape Town whose work blends journalistic clarity with heartfelt social awareness. He holds a BA in Journalism and Media from the University of Cape Town and works as a content marketer in a performance marketing agency. A writer since high school, he has published poetry and short stories in several student anthologies. His climate change poem *One Green Heart* won ArtsHelp's Global Climate Change Art Contest in 2022, and his play *Homeless, Not Heartless* was featured in the Gi60 International One Minute Play Festival in 2023. His work also appears through Shacklebound Books, West Avenue Publishing, and Wicked Shadow Press.

Maya De La Torre (she/her) is a Latina playwright and performer based in Los Angeles whose work is rooted in the belief that every story is, at its core, about love. In both writing and performance, she explores the quiet, everyday moments that hold unexpected emotional weight. She holds an MA in Classical Acting from the London Academy of Music & Dramatic Art and is a member of the Lin-Manuel Miranda Family Fellowship. Blending intimacy, lyricism, and emotional truth, Maya creates stories shaped by culture, connection, and genuine care.

Louis DeVaughn Nelson (DeVo) is a Black, Queer interdisciplinary playwright, choreographer, and dramaturg whose work has been presented in the United States, Europe, Australia, and Asia. His writing appears in blogs, anthologies, and journals, including *Obsidian: Literature & Arts in the African Diaspora*. A Dramatists Guild member and PlayPenn 2025 Cohort artist, he co-received the 2022 Carlo Annoni Prize for LGBT Plays for his translation of *Happy Reincarnation!* by Christoph Schlemmer. A 2024 NYFA Queens Art Fund grantee, DeVo lives and creates in New York City and trained at DeSales University, Drexel University, and The New School.

Matthew J. Kaplan is a Brooklyn-based playwright, filmmaker, musician, and actor rooted in the creative communities of his hometown. He wrote, produced, and directed the award-winning international short film *It's Time for Tea*. As a member of NYC's PlayGround Experiment and Brooklyn's Flatbush Community Theater, Matthew has had several one-act plays—including *Copy and Paste*, *The Invincible Eddie Vincent*, *A Haunting Melody*, and *This Is What Doctor Shapiro Was Talking About*—staged across New York City festivals. He is also a songwriter and bass player for the indie-rock band The Bright Spots.

Yangzhou (Yao) Bian is a writer and artist from Sichuan, China, a region known for its teahouses, dim sum, and vibrant street culture. She earned her B.A. and M.A. in Theatre Studies from SUNY Binghamton, where she focused on theory, criticism, and dance. Currently a Ph.D. student in Binghamton University's Translation Research and Instruction Program (TRIP), she explores transcreativity in cross-cultural theatre and interpretive originality. Her scholarship has been recognized with the Marilyn Gaddis Ross Excellence Award and the Ben Van Wyke Award for translation and research.

Melanie Payne is an author, playwright, and award-winning print and television journalist whose storytelling is shaped by a lifelong commitment to uncovering truth. After 25 years reporting for newspapers in Ohio, California, and Southwest Florida, she was recruited to an ABC affiliate in Tampa, where she led a team of enterprise and investigative reporters. Born and raised in Ohio, Melanie attended Wellesley College in Massachusetts and now resides in Florida. Her work blends journalistic rigor with theatrical imagination, bringing sharp insight and human depth to every story she tells.

Maximillian Gill is a New York–based playwright whose work has been staged by companies and festivals in the United States, Canada, the United Kingdom, and Australia. His plays include *Your Undecaying Flames* (shortlist finalist, Eugene O'Neill National Playwrights Conference), *Stay Up and Keep Rolling* (semi-finalist, Eugene O'Neill National Playwrights Conference and Premiere Stages), *Machines Eat People* (semi-finalist, Seven Devils Playwrights Conference), and *Blank Slate* (semi-finalist, Bay Area Playwrights Festival). A short film adapted from one of his monologues screened at the Tasveer South Asian Film Festival. He is a member of the New Ambassadors Theatre Company and the American Renaissance Theatre Company.

James McLindon is a New York–based playwright and member of the Nylon Fusion Theatre Company. His work has been produced and developed nationally and internationally, including at the O'Neill National Playwrights Conference—where he is a six-time semifinalist—along with Lark, PlayPenn, the Edinburgh Fringe Festival, hotINK Festival, Irish Repertory Theatre, and Victory Gardens. His plays have also been showcased by Hudson Stage Company, Abingdon, New Repertory, Lyric Stage, Detroit Rep, Great Plains Theatre Conference, Seven Devils, Ashland New Plays Festival, and Boston Playwrights Theatre. His work is published by Dramatic Publishing and Smith & Kraus.

Mark Sbani is a Denver–based playwright whose work blends sharp wit with offbeat observation. Born in New York and raised in Virginia, he later settled near the quiet lakes of Washington Park, where the rhythms of nature—especially the flowers he admires and the geese he pointedly distrusts—influence his writing. Known for his humor and distinct narrative voice, Mark crafts plays that explore the oddities and understated absurdities of everyday life. His work often reflects how small moments shape larger truths. As he jokes, "Writing a play is like strangling a goose. It takes a long time."

Achiro P. Olwoch is an award-winning writer, director, and producer from Gulu in Northern Uganda, now living in exile in New York. She is the creator of acclaimed works such as *Coffee Shop*, *Yat Madit*, and the short film *The Surrogate*. Her storytelling, rooted in questions of identity, history, and social justice, includes the novel *The End of Swahili Lines* and the play *The Survival*, which has been performed at Lincoln Center and the Perelman Performing Arts Center. A committed mentor, Achiro leads Acirocan Writes to support emerging storytellers and continues to advocate globally for LGBTQ+ rights and human rights.

Sofía Méndez Ramírez was born in Mexico City in 1999 and has been writing since childhood. At 15, she won an essay contest that led to guest presentations at FILIJ and FIL Minería. She later discovered her passion for playwriting and acting while studying Communication and Journalism at UNAM. Sofía has performed in community theaters, appeared in the short film *Yo Sentí Su Amor*, and is now pursuing an MFA in Creative Writing at Western Michigan University, where her play *That Song of Us* earned an honorable mention. Her work explores cosmovision, body-territory, and women's experiences.

Samara Siskind is a nationally and internationally produced playwright whose work appears in numerous anthologies, including *Shorter, Faster, Funnier, Great Short Comedies (Volumes 1 & 2)*, *The Best Ten-Minute Plays of 2023* and *2024*, and the Lanford Wilson New American Play Festival 2024. Her plays have been developed or produced by City Theatre Miami, Forward Theatre, tiny_Theatre, Whiskey Theatre Factory, Playwrights' Round Table, B3 Theater, Murmuration Theatre Company, Lakeshore Players Theatre, the Morgan-Wixson Theater, and Ivoryton Playhouse. Samara is the Resident Dramaturg for Athena Project and a proud member of the Dramatists Guild.

Jeremy Rafal, born in the Philippines and raised in Hawai'i, is a New York–based multi-hyphenate artist working across writing, acting, music, filmmaking, and education. His plays include *The Boy from Bantay* (FringeNYC, Flying Solo Festival), *Funhouse Funk* (NY Theater Fest, Decent Company), and *Waiting* (Take 10 Fest). His award-winning short film *Exit 15* earned Best Short Film and Best Screenplay at the Southeast Asian Film Festival and was an official selection of the SOHO International Film Festival, HAAPI Fest, and the All-Asian Independent Film Festival.

Paul Bowman is an American playwright and fiction writer whose varied life—as a farm boy, soldier, bartender, and nursing home maintenance man—shapes the grit and humanity of his work. His one-act plays have been staged in twelve U.S. states as well as in Australia and Canada, earning recognition for their sharp storytelling and emotional resonance. His fiction has appeared widely in literary journals, with twenty-one published stories and several short plays in print. Drawing from a lifetime of unconventional jobs and lived experience, Paul continues to craft plays and prose rooted in authenticity, character, and a keen sense of lived truth.

Emma Denson is a New York–based playwright and director originally from Alabama. She was a 2024 Eugene O'Neill Center New Play Conference semifinalist for *Sex and the Southeast*, and her play *Otis and Anna* won Best Short at the 2023 Downtown Urban Arts Festival. As the inaugural Drama League Rose Fellow in 2024, she traveled to London to assistant direct the stage adaptation of *Never Let Me Go* and to direct the Rose Young Company in her play *Happy Sleep*. She also recently directed her bilingual adaptation of *The Taming of the Shrew*, titled *Taming of Kate*, at Teatro Blu in Milan.